Dana Moree

Teachers on the Waves of Transformation
Czech School Culture Before and After 1989

CHARLES UNIVERSITY
KAROLINUM PRESS 2020

Originally published in Czech as *Učitelé na vlnách transformace. Kultura školy před rokem 1989 a po něm*, Prague: Karolinum, 2013

Czech edition reviewed by Prof. Dr. Miroslav Vaněk, Ph.D. (Institute of Contemporary History, Czech Academy of Sciences)
Dr. David Greger, Ph.D. (Institute for Research and Development of Education)

Faculty of Humanities, Charles University provided institutional support (FHS UK 206020/014) for the publication of this project.

Cataloguing-in-Publication Data is available from the National Library of the Czech Republic

ISBN 978-80-246-4377-9
ISBN 978-80-246-4417-2 (pdf)

Table of Contents

Acknowledgments 7

Foreword to the English edition 9

**1. The transformation of schools viewed through the lens
of contemporary theory** 11

Transformation as the creation of a new structure and culture 11

An educational system at the crossroads between the past and the future 19

School culture 25

2. Examining the transformation of school culture and the methods used 28

Interviews as the primary method 31

What the respondents didn't say: Reviewing documents 34

Parents and children 35

The researcher as a former student 37

3. About Remízek and its milieu 39

The town of Remízek 39

The stories of the Chestnut and Linden schools 40

Respondents 44

4. Teachers talk about their schools 51

The Chestnut and Linden schools before 1989 52

What was taught and how 56

Teachers as officials 58

Teachers as assessed assessors 67

Dilemmas or what the teachers would or would not stand up for 74

Relations between the teachers 85

1989 87

Mr. Brož – a new principal for Chestnut School   87
The events of 1989 at Chestnut   89
Mrs. Zemánková – the Linden School principal   99
Events of 1989 at Linden School   100
What changed after 1989   108
Society changed   109
What the reform gave and what it took away   115
Kids and parents have changed   127
Teachers after the hangover   144
The school's role in society   153
Which way forward?   160

5. Discussion and conclusions   164
Teachers against the backdrop of historical and social changes   164
Teachers' dilemmas before and after 1989   170
The transformation of the school culture   174
The transformation of the concept of education   179
Which way out of the vicious circle   186

Epilogue   192
Bibliography   194
Acts and documents   197
Summary   198
Index   201

Acknowledgments

Before I embark on this adventuresome journey of how Czech society has changed in the eyes of teachers at the Chestnut and Linden schools, I would like to thank first and foremost those who have taken the time to answer my questions. I am indebted to them for the time they spent in the interviews, as well as for their courage in lifting the veil of time to provide me with both a glimpse of the past and their invaluable reflections upon the events of the past thirty years.

I would also like to add one personal note: Not only did the teachers in Remízek teach me to read, write and count, they also showed me how to recognize true courage in today's world. Throughout the research, many teachers questioned the hero/traitor narrative. Indeed, I was able to find my answer in part thanks to them. In my view, heroism today means the courage to honestly ponder what is happening in life and to attempt to draw some conclusions from it. I am grateful to all who were willing to join me on this search.

I would also like to thank those who accompanied me through this research and listened to my findings. I am thus particularly indebted to my colleagues from the Department of Civil Society Studies at Charles University's School of Humanities, to friends who kindly and critically provided feedback on the first draft of this book and to both of my patient editors. Last but not least, I would like to thank my husband and children, who are for me an endless source of inspiration in the search for how to live in this day and age.

Foreword to the English edition

When, at the European Educational Research Conference in 2013, I first presented my findings on the changes of two small Czech schools during the transformation from the communist system to democracy, I was sure that it would be of little interest to the international public. Since my research was from a small country and on a subject that had long ceased to be topical, I felt that my audience would have a hard time fathoming it. I was sure that my Western colleagues would regard me both suspiciously and indulgently, like the time in the 1990s that I tried to explain to them that a three-course lunch was nonsense since I could live a month on its cost in a post-communist country.

But I was wrong. My audience listened extremely attentively, asking many questions. They felt a connection to teachers in my research and were compelled to ponder their own situations in relationship to them. I repeatedly experienced a similar reaction, but could not get my head around what exactly my foreign colleagues found so interesting.

One time, I could not resist the temptation to try something which ended up being a turning point in my research. I asked my audience whether they had ever said or did something that went against their inner convictions. The question was first met with absolute silence. But then hands slowly began to rise. Not one or two, but over half of the audience. I repeatedly tried out this exercise in various groups and gradually realized that even my colleagues from the democratic world experienced similar situations. Although the threat of interrogations and loss of job did not hover over them, they could imagine not doing something or, instead, doing something merely out of fear. Nothing leads us to obedience more than fear – an obedience that we do not want, but that we ultimately opt for, since disobedience would make problems for us.

It is on this principle that totalitarian society operated and continues to operate. The same holds true for democratic societies bearing totalitarian features. So, after years of contemplating the matter, I have concluded that the main difference between my experiences from a transforming post-totalitarian country and that of my colleagues from the democratic world is the speed and intensity of these changes. In the Czech Republic, we can follow the transformation from totalitarianism to democracy over the course of a single generation; all processes are apparent and apprehensible during a single human lifetime. They are therefore more concentrated, although corresponding to a certain extent with the life experiences of people living through similar phenomena, albeit in a diluted form.

I thus gradually began to see totalitarianism, like transformation and democracy, as more than pertaining to the political system. Though it is more readily visible on a central level, it begins and ends with each person who has experienced saying or doing something that he or she did not consider to be the right thing, but did it anyway out of fear.

So after many years of hesitation, I reached the conclusion that my research warranted an English translation. My initial intention was to modify the book for an English readership, but in the end I made only a few small changes to the original study so that the context could be better grasped. I would like to invite the reader to explore what causes fear in us and how we can free ourselves from it within the structure of our everyday lives. This will all be examined within the framework of two small Czech schools that went through the final phase of the communist regime, the ferment of the period around the 1989 revolution and the transition to that which we somewhat brazenly call democracy.

1. The transformation of schools viewed through the lens of contemporary theory

Transformation as the creation of a new structure and culture

In this chapter we will attempt to outline how a school's culture, and thus its transformation,[1] related to the transformation of society as a whole, or, in other words, why there is also the need to examine the change of its culture within the context of society's transformation. This starting point is crucial for understanding the research and for interpreting its results.

Now thirty years down the road of the transformation's start, we can look back and reflect upon some of the processes that were not necessarily apparent to us as the transformation was underway. It's not always possible to clearly assess from the ship itself how straight or zigzagging the journey has been, how many obstacles have been avoided, how many times the crew has been disgruntled or pleased with the captain's decisions. This can only be evaluated after a sufficient distance has been covered. I feel that thirty years is long enough to begin to reflect upon the journey taken and learn from what has or has not happened.

Numerous books and articles have been written on the transformation of central and eastern Europe (Kollmorgen, 2011, provides, for instance, a thorough overview of various types of theories and reflects upon their development). As a starting point for my own work, a few main postulates from these books are worth mentioning.

In 1989, when the countries of central and eastern Europe began their transformation process, the pressure from the start was primarily on the

---

1 The term "transformation" will be used here for the post-1989 period, especially when changes that occurred in society are examined. The term "post-communism" will be used to describe this period. The period up to 1989 will be called "communist" in accordance with the use by Holmes (1997), who argued that though it was not a real communist system, it was the declared objective that the system was striving for.

restructuring of these societies. There was the need to find a safe way to shift from a centrally planned economy to decentralization, to distribute state property among companies and groups of citizens and to change communist legislation into democratic laws, among many other things. Every country took a slightly different path, though the task at hand was similar for all of them.

Yet restructuring is not something that occurs outside the realm of culture and without cultural changes. Successful restructuring also requires cultural changes that are not undertaken after the restructuring is finished. On the contrary, the cultural change, the change in paradigm, the change in how things are done and, above all, a culture's ideas of how things should be done in a new way, are a catalyst for these structural changes. Ideas form in the people's minds of what these new structures should look like; ideas form in a culture of what a new world should look like and what to do with the old one. According to the publications written on this subject, it seems that this very point became problematic and led to, among other things, a certain anomie that societies of central and eastern Europe, including the Czech Republic, are currently experiencing.

After 1989, the societies of central and eastern Europe underwent a transformation phase that Sztompka defines as a change in the society as a whole, and not a partial change within the current society The great driving force of this change was the desire to westernize, to return to the West (Berend, 2009; Sztompka, 1993). Various writers understood this return to the West in different ways. Sztompka (1993) asks where exactly we're returning to. Is our final destination a European house or a European home? At first glance, the difference between these two words may not be great, but the means by which this return is undertaken is, in his view, radically different. In short, we can move into a European house – get a decree, the right to a flat, gather up our things, load them into trucks and take them there. The formal right to this cannot be questioned; everyone must accept it. However, a return to the European home means assuming the basic responsibilities of this home – not only for its formal existence, but also for its quality. It means a willingness to take part in its development, to negotiate our common interests with neighbors, to tend to our relationships with them and once again to slowly grow together with them. Building a home is work based on minor interactions, symbolic exchanges and a willingness to listen. And yet it seems that some kind of dissonance and disharmony occurred here.

Indeed, culture has a certain inertia. Changing the backdrop – if we can metaphorically express political changes in this way – does not necessarily mean a change in the character of the actors or a change of script. Sztompka (1993) introduces the term "the boomerang effect" to describe this phenomenon. In his view, people adopted behavior prior to 1989 that impeded the development of socialism during the "normalization" period of hard-line communism in the 1970s and 80s, only to have the same type of behavior impede the development of capitalism following 1989. What specific traits were these? Though various authors differ in listing them, they agree on the essential points: People were used to having security, indoctrination, little money and no great risks. Moreover, everyone looked down on people from the business world (Berend, 2009: 198). However, according to Sztompka (1993), building a democratic system requires, above all, a business culture based on, among other things, a willingness to take risks, and a civic culture based on the development of a civic society and civic responsibility, which we will get to later. Prior to 1989 there was no way of practicing these traits or skills, and yet these were the very things needed to build or, rather, rebuild the old world into a new world. So what was to be done?

In the early years, the basic inspiration was the way the established democracies worked in the West. Several factors played a role here. With the fall of the Iron Curtain certain new developments also took place in the West. Some authors even see the start of globalization in the context of this historical moment. Great pressure was placed on expanding existing structures such as the European Union and NATO. This obviously required that the laws and structures in post-communist countries be aligned with the international norm. Yet this international norm arose as a result or product of a certain culture, and differed from that which was the driving force in post-communist countries. Berend (2009: 197) characterizes this fact: "People and their politicians admired the attractive consumerism, ample supply of goods and high living standards, but overlooked the high prices, the work ethic, and the efficiency that created it." Thus a certain disillusionment with the transformation process took place. Given the great social downturn in the early post-1989 years, the dream of full shops and of the possibility to buy anything began to recede and seemed practically out of reach (Berend, 2009). This downswing arrived in various countries at a different speed – the first economic depression didn't hit the Czech Republic until after 1997. Nevertheless, the change in the feeling of social security sooner or later impacted and divided the population into those who were able to grasp the new opportunities and those who weren't. Faith in a rapid change and a rapid obtainment of a Western standard of living began to wobble, and the willingness to undertake structural changes, shaken by this distrust, often merely led to a kind of "Potemkin harmonization" (Berend, 2009) or, in the words of the slogan often used by teachers to describe the reform of the education system, "having your cake and eating it to." (Moree, 2008).

Berend (2009) even speaks of a social shock that he characterizes as a cultural affair. The market economy was forced upon a society that was culturally different. The cultural concept prior to 1989 remained and, combined with the market economy, resulted in something that was unsatisfactory for much of the population.

Another significant matter that remains unresolved is the need for the very linking of the idea of democracy with a market economy. Evident in many writings is a kind of conditioning of one by the other (Berend, 2009). Others, however, do not automatically draw a direct line between a free market and political transformation (Sztompka, 1993).

What about culture then? The thing about culture is that it's always linked to a time, to a certain period. It can change and it is changing, yet this change occurs slowly. Culture changes in a kind of inertia that takes on new forms. Kennedy (2002) even claims that the very process of transformation produced a new culture that was neither totalitarian nor democratic, but transitional. A transition culture is then defined as a "contradiction in the very term. A culture includes values, convictions, symbols and rituals, while a transition is a change in a political and economic system [...] A transition culture is thus a mobilizing culture organized around certain logical and normative oppositions, valuations of expertise, and interpretations of history that provide a basic framework for change." (Kennedy, 2002: 8).

Nevertheless, a culture has many layers and the question is which of its components changes at what rate. Does a culture change as a whole, or is the existence of that which Kennedy (2002) calls a transition culture possible for the very reason that the various components change at a different rate and order?

We know from writings on the subject that the great theme in the transformation process is the change in the value system. The transformation process brought with it two important consequences in this respect. This consisted of a certain **undermining of the value system**, which ceased to provide orientation for everyday life (Holmes, 1997). An oft repeated premise was that anything would be better than the ways things were run prior to 1989 (Buraway – Verdery, 1999). Often the sentiment that everything must be different was the only thing that everyone agreed on (Dahrendorf, 2005).

The question of trust became an important matter: Who and what could be trusted? The transforming political system no longer provided a clear explanation of the world and for many people the state remained enemy number one. Trust continued to be linked more with personal relations, yet beyond that almost nothing was to be trusted.

Marková (2004) recalls in this context the concept of the *homeless mind*, defined as the feeling of existential solitude and destitution. The homeless mind is not a phenomenon necessarily linked to transformation situations. This term was first introduced by Berger in 1973. "When people began to forge their own individual identities and when their expectations of social recognition of these new identities were not fulfilled, the desired freedom brought with it a feeling of loneliness and isolation." (Marková, 2004: 17).

This feeling of loneliness probably wouldn't have been so severe had the people not faced a situation that had no solution *a priori*. Marková (2004) points out that democracy necessarily requires the capacity for dialogue. Yet socialization in the totalitarian[2] world meant attempting a monologist interpretation of the world that was also changing throughout life just as the totalitarian regime itself was changing. In all of its shapes – whether its more brutal form of the 1950s or in the more moderate one of the late 1980s – there prevailed the feeling that human life is influenced by many factors, of which only a few are predictable and can by influenced. People lived in a double reality (Marková, 2004; Moree, 2008) and could, in Marková's view, react to it in two ways: either by conforming to it or as part of the dissent. "The safest conformist strategy when dealing with the situation was to avoid any meaningful communication or self-expression, and to refuse any responsibility for one's world." (Marková, 2004: 40).

However, building a democracy after 1989 required a willingness to assume responsibility and to be open to dialogue. Given that the engrained ways of behaving and relationships are considerably inert and do not change over the course of a person's life as quickly as a political

---

2 I am using in this book the term "totalitarian" to describe the pre-1989 regime, mainly because that is how the respondents spoke about the regime.

regime (Marková, 2004), the post-revolutionary euphoria instead gave way to a feeling of decline, chaos, anomie and solitude.

It was in this vacuum of values that the people's expectations of public figures, of leaders, then radically increased. Society needed to acquire some kind of orientation and, in its instilled helpless way, expected that this orientation would come to them from above (Dahrendorf, 2005; Holmes, 1997).

Consequently, most of the authors agree that a condition for a successful transformation is, above all, a combination of structural changes and cultural changes, changes in people's attitudes and civic harmony, which both enables this change and augments it (Berend, 2009; Holmes, 1997; Kennedy, 2002; Dahrendorf, 2005 and others). Yet several steps first need to be taken before we can start the change in culture. First and foremost, we need to understand the cultural changes that occurred over the past thirty years. Since the society we live in is stratified and consists of many groups, such a change cannot be described in categories covering the entire society. Actually it can, but since we do not presently know enough about the qualitative parameters for such vast research, we first have to focus on a few specific groups that have experienced the change and, only then, after formulating theories, can we further examine using a broader sampling of society and quantitative methods. We therefore need to choose a target group for this preliminary explorative research of a qualitative nature.

If we postulate that a genuine and deep transformation cannot be achieved without a cultural change in the realm of citizenship, we must first contemplate the characteristics of citizenship. We need to know how to characterize the coveted goal of this change and which target groups should be chosen for this exploratory research.

The question at hand is then how do we recognize a person-citizen capable of building a democratic system. Some research conducted in recent years in western countries show the need to distinguish between several aspects of such citizenship. Everyone agrees that a good citizen should be a decent person who obeys the laws. There's little doubt that this is true, yet just being a decent person does not suffice for building a democracy. What is also needed is the ability to imagine how to actively fill the space of the freedom created, and a willingness to become involved on a certain level, to take part in building the world in which we live (Oser – Veugelers, eds., 2008; Veugelers, ed., 2011).

Prior research showed that there are two types of involvement in society. Westheimer writes that there are three types of citizens: a personally responsible citizen, who will take part in a wide range of voluntary activities and is available to those in distress or facing a difficult situation in life. A participating citizen is, above all, active in society and civic initiatives on a local, regional or state-wide level. A citizen is oriented toward social justice and capable of critical assessment of social, political and economic structures. He or she examines strategies of how to change these structures (Westheimer in Oser – Veugelers, 2008: 20–21).

Besides these measurable parameters of involvement, there are also more subtle levels of citizenship that are no less important for life in a democratic society. Kymlicka (2001) reflected upon how to arrange things so that all citizens in a society felt good. Obviously a certain system – a legal system – needed to be established. But that was not enough to create a good feeling. Something more was needed in his concept, something called *civility*. What does that look like? Not only do I have the right to enter a shop, cinema, pharmacy and the likes, but I also feel good and welcomed there. How is such a feeling created? Through the smile of a shop assistant, through a short, informal chat about the weather or selection of products, by relinquishing one's seat on the tram with a smile and not a disdainful grimace. Civility is formed in the atmosphere and delicate web or relationships in a public space. Yet it also depends on a feeling of security and trust. However, in a transforming society the very undermining of certainties complicates even everyday human civility in a public space.

Although all this may appear banal at first glance, actually doing it requires absolute engagement, an endless ability to reflect upon what is occurring in one's immediate surroundings and well contemplated decision-making. Such behavior needs to be developed in life, and instilled and requires practice. Kymlicka posed the question of where such behavior can be taught so that its further development is guaranteed in society. He came up with two suggestions. One such milieu where people practiced this *civility* could be the civic society organization whose objectives were essentially to create a space for this type of citizenship. Unfortunately, not all civic society organizations are truly democratic; there are a number of associations and movements that are of an undemocratic nature. Moreover, not all citizens unite or even become involved in such organizations. The other possibility is quite logically the school, which should guide students toward becoming citizens in the true meaning of the word. Citizens, who will not only passively observe laws, but also actively take part in building a deeply humane society.

If we accept the premise that schools are crucial for building a civic society and thus also for transforming the entire society, the curtains to a very tense drama opens before us. Prior to 1989, schools were, at least according to the official documents, the very place where the ideal socialist citizen – the *homo sovieticus* – was to be produced (Kozakiewicz, 1992). They were then suddenly supposed to become a place to create models through which children would learn to create a free society.

Here we encounter a number of possible obstacles and uncertainties. What happens in such a situation to the convictions of teachers? How do they change and why? How do they perceive these changes and how do they change their behavior, their definition of themselves as teachers and their roles in society. What dilemmas does this new situation produce? These seem to be fundamental questions, especially if we take into account that children cannot learn democratic citizenship in an undemocratic environment (Westheimer in Oser – Veugelers, 2008; Banks, 2004). For instance, if a school decides to teach democratic citizenship and the teachers and students do not experience a democratic culture within their microcosm, they most likely won't achieve anything – regardless of the curriculum. The school culture – the fragile web of symbols, rituals, values, relationships and stories (Banks, 2004; Higgins – Sadh, 1998; Veugelers, 2007; Peterson – Deal, 2009 and others) – is a decisive factor for practicing civic skills.

The transformation of schools – just like the transformation of a society – must take place in synchronicity with many different processes. The restructuring and change of a culture are a necessary condition (Fullan, 2000; Holmes, 1997). This process of change then is not typical just for post-communist countries. A revision of education's place in the lives of western societies has been ongoing over the past fifty years. In this sense, we are not alone on this trek, but belong to a specific thought current that reflects the fermentation of contemporary times in education (Giroux – McLaren, eds. 1989; Veugelers, ed. 2011).

Owing to the random composition of teachers and students (or parents) that represent various groups living in one area, schools reflect events in the broader society (Kutsyuruba, 2011). This provides us with an ideal sample for researching the transformation.

In the mirror of changes of the school culture we can try to describe what happened in our world and, above all, where to focus on its further development. Yet before anything else, we should take a look at two aspects that are crucial for understanding the monitored research: the school culture and the transformation of the educational system in the Czech Republic.

An educational system at the crossroads between the past and the future

We understand transformation as the movement from one state of things to another. It therefore makes sense to begin then with what we know for certain about the educational system prior to 1989.

The main goal of education was uniform: to produce a socialist citizen. This goal was declared both in the methodological materials for teachers and in the textbooks themselves. We see this, for instance, in a didactic and methodological book for first-form students: "The pupils should acquire the first simple, age-adequate ideas of our socialist society and the foundation for the development of socialist and international sentiments." (Tupý – Vlčková – Nečesaná – Dušková, 1975: 8). In the foreword to a civics textbook for the sixth grade of basic school, this goal is explained: "You are learning that the basis for all wealth and development of our country is the sacrificial and dignified work of the people, who, under the leadership of the Czechoslovak Communist Party, are building a socialist society. You are understanding that the main guarantee for the construction of this society are educated, expertly prepared, politically conscious and active citizens." (Jelínková – Prusáková, 1988: 7).

The entire educational system was subordinate to this goal: The state had absolute control over the individual types of schools (Kozakiewicz, 1992) – there were no private schools or schools affiliated with a religion. The state also had control over the teaching curriculum (Tomusk, 2001). This also obviously meant complete control over books (Cerych, 1997; Kozakiewicz, 1992; Szebenyi, 1992; Walterová – Greger, 2006). If we wanted for the sake of clarity to put this extent of control in numbers we'd only have to glimpse the list of writers taught in literature textbooks for the 4th year of secondary schools from 1978, 1987 and 2004. After 1989, the list increased by nearly forty names and many other writers were removed from the list (see Moree, 2008). Forbidden literature also obviously existed. But it is interesting that many claim that there was no official list of such literature. Urbášek (2011: 460), for instance, states that lists of forbidden writers were read out at meetings, but that no one was allowed to take notes. Everyone had "to know", who they were not allowed to quote or otherwise refer to.

Prior to 1989, the educational system was based mainly on apprentice schools – as late as 1990 over 60% of children ended up at secondary vocational schools (Berend, 2009: 227).

In addition to this control over the structure and content, available information shows that the state also attempted to maintain control over the loyalty of teachers, which is why applicants to the teachers' college had to be thoroughly screened (Ulc, 1978).

The chance to further one's education was a prominent topic during communism, as was the extent to which a family's political profile influenced this possibility. Both teachers and students had to deal with this. In cases of children from working-class families, positive discrimination, as Urbášek tersely calls it in the book by Vaněk et al. (2011), was applied. Wong (1998: 16) maintains that by doing so "the Czechoslovak Communist Party contributed to the active stratification of society and to the generational imbalance." The employment of the parents at the time did not influence this selection (e.g. many of the Charta 77 signatories were blue-collar workers); the proletarian lineage of the ancestors was decisive.

We have relatively detailed knowledge of the situation at universities where, according to Urbášek (in Vaněk, 2011), teachers in the 1970s were divided into four groups based on political reliability. The most reliable had a relatively open door to a career; the less reliable could not achieve a higher title than doctorate of science. Faster promotions or at least security was provided to those willing to take part in building the regime in the form of, for instance, communist party membership.

Finding clear proof of this is very complicated since the guidelines and other such documents for choosing applicants for various types of schools were carefully concealed. Exceptions do, however, appear. More specific information was published in the 1970s in the exile periodical *Listy* (December 1974). We read here that those applying to study at law schools were divided into five categories: 1) communist party members; 2) those whose parents are party members; 3) children of important representative of other parties; 4) children with a proletarian lineage and 5) others. The fifth category did not include children of former communist party members, because their parents had already demonstrated a lack of loyalty to the regime.

The question arises of how the teachers acted in this constricted system. In every regime, education represents a primary socialization tool and respondents are found who avowedly admit that education was under considerable supervision (Urbášek, 2011). Totalitarianism imposed on teachers' requirements concerning their everyday actions and there was no way of avoiding them. Teachers were constantly having to resolve some kind of dilemma – if their convictions did not completely match the regime's requirements. Obviously, as Vaněk writes (2011), in researching the behavior during totalitarianism it should be understood that not everyone automatically took an interest in politics. In every regime there are people who simply don't concern themselves with it. But even those not interested in politics were at least sometimes confronted with its demands. As we will see later in this book, teachers dealt with dilemmas they encountered in their everyday professional life in various ways and, twenty years later, have various views of these experiences.

One of the reasons why I feel it important to ask teachers about their work during the communist regime is that we know from other works that totalitarian regimes in particular push for teachers to be visibly incorporated into the system and for them to appear as the regime's active supporter. Teachers' activities during the period of Nazism have already been described in detail. Lansing (2010) writes that three characteristics can be noticed with teachers: they were forced to become members of various professional organizations that were linked to the regime; they were denounced for various reasons – e.g. for membership in a church; and – lastly – teachers usually accepted this type of coercion. For instance, in Nazi Germany teachers filled out questionnaires on the racial makeup of their families.

Based on autobiographical interviews of a group of sociologists, Konopásek (2000) observes that two levels were apparent in relation to the Czechoslovak Communist Party: an existential level in which it was truly about values and worldview, and an existence level in which it was simply about 'survival' and providing the best possible material conditions for oneself and one's family. The younger the respondents, the more prevalent the existence level in relation to the Czechoslovak Communist Party.

In my view, one other fact needs to be underscored here. That people behave differently under duress and also differently assess the degree of danger is a given. None of us know how we would act under the conditions that teachers experienced in Czechoslovakia in the 1970s and 80s. I feel that, given the theme of transformation, an assessment of their conduct and personal decisions is irrelevant. If, however, we assert that teachers are important players in a society's transformation in the sense that they support a democratic type of citizenship, we have to ask them how they view their experiences in retrospect, what conclusions they have drawn from them, if their stories are part of the events in the school and if they thus ensure a certain historic and intergenerational exchange or whether they are made taboo. How traumatic experiences are handled after their completion is for the future health of the individuals and even society as a whole perhaps even more important than whether a traumatic event occurred. This is the very reason why we must ask about the real experiences and reflect upon them not only in the context of the communist regime at that time, but also at present when they can serve as valuable material for forming the future.

We can therefore surmise from the above that there were many reasons for the transformation of the education system in 1989. These reasons can be divided into external (international) and internal (domestic). To change the educational system on the internal level there is always the need to synchronize that which occurs in the direction from the center (at the level of the government, ministries, etc.) downwards – i.e. towards the individual schools and teachers – with the changes initiated by individual teachers and schools. Ultimately, they can even change the central level. Fullan (1996) thus distinguishes between the *top-down* and *bottom-up approach*. If the change is initiated only at the top and is unable to convince teachers of its importance, a real change cannot occur anyway. Every change therefore lies on the shoulders of specific teachers, who either implement or do not implement it during their classroom work. If teachers do not believe in the essence of the change and do not see any sense in it, there is little hope in its implementation. We also know that teachers are always to a certain extent resistant to change (Goodson, 2005; Fullan, 2000). Indeed, change brings a certain instability, an extra exertion, and a strain is needed for teachers to be willing to invest their time and energy into an actual change. Nevertheless, teachers are the first group that regimes take aim at in the 'fight over the young'.

From the transformations in other post-communist countries we know that during the first years many did not make changes in the curriculum (Silova, 2005). What's more, some changes are made just for appearance's sake and can greatly differ from the original plan (Silova, 2005).

Another valid question is on which side the changes are initiated and from where in the transformation process inspiration is drawn. Where is the idea formed regarding what the changed educational system should look like?

An important slogan of social transformation during the first few years after 1989 was 'back to Europe'. Much of the inspiration thus logically came from other countries; teachers as well as ministry workers travelled to other countries to see how things worked and tried to apply examples of good practices. International influences on the domestic policy or even actions in specific schools are called the "travelling policy" (Bahry, 2005; Jones – Alexiadou, 2001; Ozga – Jones, 2006; Sedon, 2005). Perhaps the notion that not only people and goods travel in a globalized world, but also ideas, is not surprising, and this is what happened in the Czech Republic after 1989. It is typical of a travelling policy that there is no way to examine the results, and that the paths of the ideas are often poorly mapped. An idea coming from abroad can take root on a central level and travel from there in the form of changed laws or decrees to the individual regions and schools, where they somehow take hold – sometimes merely formally, "so that they can have their cake and eat it too". Elsewhere it falls on fertile soil. A travelling policy can also first make its way to a certain school where it might be successfully implemented without central support. These movements obviously increase the system's disparateness. The lesser the movement and communication in a *top-down* and *bottom-up* direction, the greater the probability of chaos.

Context plays a great role in whether a change is truly implemented or not. Goodson and Hargreaves (1996) speak about the key role of context and of individuals, which are points often omitted. It often occurs in the transformation process that teachers, who at the start of their careers usually have ideals, a great desire to teach and to accompany children as they grow, are gradually overwhelmed with technical requirements and administrative tasks to the point that their ideals fade. Exhausted and worn out, they retire with the feeling that they were unable to fulfil their ideals. Therefore, in introducing changes it is important not to forget about the context, historical memory and work with individuals.

After 1989, the educational system, among other things, underwent a transformation in the Czech Republic. Immediately following the regime change, the education law of 1984 (Act 171/1990 Coll.) was considerably amended. This amendment enabled, above all, the creation of private and religious schools. During the first decade, three types of educational programs for basic schools were created: the National School, Primary School and Elementary School. While this initial phase of the transformation was very spontaneous, the second phase, roughly corresponding to the period around the Czech Republic's entrance into the European Union, had been planned for many years.

Czech education waited until 2004 for the new school law (Act no. 561/2004 Coll., on pre-school, basic, secondary, tertiary vocational and other education). This law predominantly transformed the curriculum and work methods in schools. A centrally planned curriculum was replaced by general educational programs (RVP, rámcový vzdělávací program), based on which each school created its own school educational program (ŠVP, školní vzdělávací program). These had to be drawn up by the teachers themselves at each school; we know from prior research that the process of writing the ŠVPs required different dynamics at each school. At some schools it was a chance to brain storm over how to newly structure the curriculum. Elsewhere, the creation of an educational program represented increased administrative pressure and burden without financial remuneration, and led to a deterioration of relations between people. Almost everywhere teachers agree that the administrative burden has significantly increased in recent years (Moree, 2008).

Even though the new school law did not see the light of day until nearly fifteen years after the political changes had begun, it does not mean that nothing was happening until that time. In addition to the aforementioned first amendment school law from 1990, the White Book (the National Program for Education) was drafted in 2001. Yet for such a fundamental area as education undoubtedly is, all the changes, their faltering attempts and uncertain direction led to a paradoxical situation. Although educational reform was carried out, no bridge between the new school law and general educational programs was created, even though the school law promised this in paragraph 3. It was thereby intended to become the National Educational Program, which was to establish an overall vision, and the education goals and was to serve in a decentralized system as a fixed point of orientation for schools in forging their own school educational programs. Schools thus teach according to de-centralized school educational programs without a clear orientation regarding content and without a distinct definition of what is considered to be basic education in the Czech Republic (Moree, 2008).

Although there were changes in the structure, the question is to what extent they were truly implemented, and especially how much they influenced actions in schools. Therefore, a combination of structural and cultural changes is crucial for both the social transformation, as well as for changes in the educational system (Fullan, 2000). It is important how that fragile web of invisible context, which we call the school culture and which is essential for the success of the democratization process, is changed. The context, and how people feel in an environment where they spend nearly a third of their days is an important indicator of what can genuinely be changed in a society. Although it is important, civility is difficult to gauge in schools. This is the very area we will look at next.

School culture

In examining school culture, let us begin with a statement by Veugelers (2006: 235): "Education does not merely prepare students for society. Rather, society is already present in the school in the form of the curriculum, teachers and students." Parents, children, teachers and staff create in schools a micro-society, which generally is not divided by social status, health status and other indicators. Children, their parents and teachers meet randomly in schools, spending much time together there and forming their own culture. This culture is obviously influenced by the cultures that individuals (students, parents and teachers) bring from their homes to this group.

A school's culture can be examined from a wide array of viewpoints; we can choose methods from a broad range of social sciences – from anthropology to sociology (Pol et al. 2006). In this study we will view all participants in the school culture as beings that jointly form the group whose culture can be described. A school's culture is characterized by the number of indicators and parameters that help us examine and analyze it. Yet it is important to realize that a culture is never neutral (Hinde, 2004). It always positively or negatively influences what happens in a school, either as an accelerator or as an engaged handbrake that has been forgotten.

Two terms, often used interchangeably, exist to describe the fragile web of relationships, rituals, shared meanings and contents: *hidden curriculum* and *civitas*. Klaassen (1992) mainly understands a hidden curriculum as the way teachers acquaint children with the material presented in classrooms. This is a combination of the choice of e.g. curriculum content and the methods, class management, atmosphere, and language that the teacher and students use. This primarily concerns factors that are outside the curriculum of a given subject, but that fundamentally influence how and what children are taught.

Klaassen (1992) has a broader interpretation of school culture in that it entails the entire school milieu and all those involved, exceeding the borders of the individual classes. I will adhere to Klaassen's classification in this study.

Most writers agree that **relationships** are key for a school's culture, both those between teachers and those between teachers and students (Higgens – Sadh, 1998). Relationships leading to a friendly environment facilitate cooperation and fundamentally impact what happens throughout a school. I should mention here one of many examples from my Czech experiences. At a seminar organized as part of the further education of teachers, I sought along with teachers a topic for the discussion part of a course using the *World Café* method. There were some twenty teachers from all parts of the Czech Republic in the room, generally one from every school. When I asked which theme they'd like to discuss, one teacher answered that he wanted to discuss bullying. I began by asking who was bullying whom. There followed an avalanche of responses from teachers shouting each other down: teachers bully students, student bully teachers, principals bully teachers and teachers bully principals. One teacher summed it up by declaring that everyone bullies everyone. Only one teacher contributed to the discussion by saying that she felt like a Martian because at her school there was no bullying, but instead a positive atmosphere that everyone enjoyed being a part of. She truly represented the exception in the entire group.

Similar experiences led me to the conclusion that relations are important for understanding the overall situation at schools; questions regarding cooperation among teachers can, for instance, help us analyze them (Hargreaves, 1994; Kutsyuruba, 2011). Another indicator of relations is the figure of the principal. Much depends on whether he or she is an inspirational workhorse or instead remains in the background and runs the school in a kind of inertia (Peterson – Deal, 2009).

Other important indicators for school culture are **visions and values**. Visions relate to a feeling of meaning, with a direction and orientation towards the future. Values refer to what is appreciated and perceived as valuable (Peterson - Deal, 2009). Yet from an anthropological perspective values are an extremely complex category that has no simple and clear definition. They refer to a kind of previously determined curriculum that is, however, "beyond people."

Since in this research I am mainly trying to comprehend specific individuals in specific situations and use them to show fundamental categories, I will focus more on dilemmas. This also corresponds to some intervention models in which values are linked to specific dilemmas-situations, i.e. situations in which those affected must decide between two possibilities (Bittl – Moree, 2010).

Other aspects of school culture are **rituals and symbols** (Peterson – Deal, 2009), which are activities that are repeated in school such as ceremonies and awards to students and teachers, and how they are performed. All external attributes, such as the decoration of a school, its equipment and furnishings, as well as the openness of a school to the public and its means of relating to external world is part of this (Hinde, 2004; Pol et al., 2006).

The stories and history of a school create a feeling of continuity or discontinuity as the case may be. A view to the past provides a signal of how to deal with current situations. The ability to learn from the past allows us to avoid the same mistakes (Peterson – Deal, 2009). Present-day events in schools can then be transformed into stories of success or of failure. Even the kind of story (success or failure) that teachers and students prefer to tell about a school speaks volumes about the school culture (Hinde, 2004).

Higgins – Sadh (1998) also speaks of the **existence of normative expectations** of a school as a whole and of the individuals. One question is then to what extent these perceived expectations are in accordance with the visions and values of individuals, and to what extent they instead stand in contrast.

School culture always exists and strongly influences how individuals feel in an environment and what kind of results they achieve. School culture can help the educational process, but it can also do considerable damage to it. Peterson – Deal (2009) introduces the term **toxic culture** for such a case. This differs in all conceivable parameters from a positive culture. We can characterize it as the sum of a lack of vision, the destructive stories that people tell amongst themselves, a focus on negative relationships and on a feeling of failure. This concerns all possible types of interactions and hidden messages that, although subliminal, nevertheless or possibly therefore create the overall impression of a disconnection between people and the feeling of looming or actual failure. A toxic culture negatively influences relations, the professionalism of individuals and the entire group's performance.

2. Examining the transformation of school culture and the methods used

The context described above indicates the specifics of the research focused on the transformation of school culture in the post-communist milieu. I will now try to summarize some points that are crucial in choosing the research questions and methods.

In a country that rapidly transformed from a totalitarian regime into one that is more open, teachers do indeed find themselves in a unique situation. Esteve (2000) compares this situation to a stage where the actors play their roles and then in the middle of the play somebody changes the background scenery. The audience is the same, the performance continues, the script remains unaltered, and yet everything is different. How do the actors manage this change? Do they start to look for a culprit? Do they end the performance? Do they call for a break and then agree on how to continue? Do they carry on as if nothing happened? These are some of the questions that can certainly arise when examining what teachers experienced in 1989, to what extent the society-wide changes affected specific schools and what kind of stories of schools were formed following these political changes up until the present day. Another obvious question is whether teachers experienced 1989 as a real turning point or whether the key events of their professional life occurred at other times.

A change of background in the middle of a performance also clearly influences relations and the entire symbolic and ritual world. Some symbols have disappeared. What replaced them, who decided on whether the place would remain vacant, who refilled it and how? Which values helped create all of this? Which dilemmas reappeared? And how were these changes projected into relations on all conceivable levels?

We know from international writings that there are specific ways to examine school environments. Part of this is the fact that social transformation creates an environment that research has difficulties expressing. The transformation experience is so malleable, heterogeneous and mutable that it requires specific methods (Buraway – Verdery, 1999; Konopásek, 2000). Konopásek writes that the main source of inspiration in examining transforming realities is the narration of stories. Here he agrees with Gardner (2003), who asserts that narrative is a way of linking the past to the future. This is not a case of reconstructing a history that attempts to provide an objective and true picture of everything that took place. Narration creates an image of a "lived and shared historical experience" (Gardner, 2003: 178).

According to Goodson (2008: 3) the profession of teachers is "politically and socially constructed"; this is the very reason why we tend to perceive them as either culprits or victims of social changes. Along with having their own public identity, teachers have a certain latent identity in the form of political views, convictions and attitudes that then influences the way they work in the public role of teachers. This latent identity needs to be recognized and examined (Goodson, 2008), and here too narrative research proves to be a key method.

The testimonies of teachers are therefore a primary source of information. Yet it is important to maintain the tension between the two lines of force when working with their narratives. Teachers must be able to freely recount their stories so that their narratives become as complex as possible. In this, interviewing teachers approximates the oral-history method – i.e. unimpeded biographical narratives in which there are often repeated interview sessions between the researcher and the respondent (Vaněk – Mücke, 2011). Yet the narrative must also be structured so that it provides responses to the research questions.

When researching schools, narration as a primary source of information must be accompanied by other sources – historical and other printed materials, school documents, etc. (Goodson, 2008). Burgesse (1985) asserts that it is of the utmost importance to permanently link life stories to historical context. Context combined with the narratives of the various participants then creates the narrative of a given school. Here it is important to seek the critical incidents (Goodson – Anstead, 2012) that brought about the fundamental turn in events at a specific school.

Last but not least, a profound reflection upon the narrative of the research itself occurs. The researcher experiences his or her own story with the researched environment, and this too is a valuable source of information for the final analysis (Trahar, 2009). This factor corresponds to the basic postulates of educational anthropology.

Before I justify the choice of methods for my work, I will introduce prior research on school culture conducted in the Czech Republic. This past research mainly shows a certain partiality and does not meet all of the aforementioned criteria. Although some of the research attempts to include a greater number of schools, their methodology is reduced to a questionnaire that is insufficient, despite the effort to capture the school culture and its environment. Urbášek (in Vaněk, 2009) presents interviews with numerous university teachers. Yet these interviews are removed from the social context in which the teachers work. The researched teachers worked at different schools, and therefore it was not possible to verify their view of a situation and to acquire in the end a more complex picture that might have resulted from someone at the same school giving a completely different view of a specific situation.

In structuring the research, these arguments led me to the following premises and methods:

1) For the research to be successful, I was going to have to work with **schools** where the teachers really wanted to **focus** on a given topic. However, past experience from research in Czech schools generally shows that it is extremely difficult to get an entire school to cooperate with the research, especially if it concerns such a thorny issue as social and political changes related to education, their influence on what happens in schools and even on the biographies of the individual teachers. I therefore chose a milieu where I already knew the teachers and they knew me; this often proved to be the only possible way in many interviews. Many of the teachers told me during the interviews that they wouldn't have been willing to speak about similar subjects if they had not known me and trusted me.

2) I promised my respondents that they would remain **anonymous**. All names and titles are changed during the analysis process. I made up a fictional name for the town and called the schools Chestnut and Linden. The basic information about the milieu is accurate; the description is generalized so that the place cannot be precisely identified. This also applies for the names of teachers involved in the book, and there is no system by which they can be decoded (e.g. the first letter of the real names are the same as the names in the book, etc.). In analyzing the interviews I decided to use the altered names and not to refer to the respondents as x or y. This allowed me to better demonstrate the complexity of their stories. This strict **anonymity** is an expression of gratitude for the faith the respondents showed me in sharing their stories.

3) I employed a **combination of several methods** for my research. I supplemented my teacher interviews with a study of documents from both schools (these were annual reports or entries in local chronicles). It was mainly due to the data on how many children prior to 1989 received negative marks influencing their educational paths that the research also included an analysis of documents from the district archive.

4) **Triangulation** was then also achieved in both researched schools. Both schools allowed me to speak with parents as part of the parent-teacher meetings in 2012; this research was also supplemented by Higgins-D'Alessandro – Sadh (1998) type questionnaires gauging school culture. Respondents were sixth-grade students in both schools. Though these materials are more of a supplementary nature, they augment the teachers' responses and in many ways provide important information on the context of both schools.

5) For the duration of the research I kept a **field journal** that included telephone numbers of the individuals taking part in the research, records concerning the context in which the interviews were held, and the final phase of authorization of the statements used.

6) Four **research questions** were formulated that have support in the theoretical concepts already presented:
   a) Which historical/social changes influence teachers in their work?
   b) What dilemmas do these changes bring?
   c) How did the transformation influence school culture and especially relations in schools (between teachers, teachers and principals, teachers and students)?
   d) How did the transformation influence the concept of school and the goals of education?

I combined methods to seek responses to these research questions. In the case of the interviews, I created a script directly derived from these questions; for some aspects I employed concretization in interviewing the teachers (e.g. questions concerning school reforms), which is why there are two more interview questions than research questions.

Interviews as the primary method

The most important research method are the interviews with the individual teachers. For the interviews at Chestnut School I began with the older generation of teachers – i.e. those with whom I already had a personal relationship and who were teaching at the school when I attended it as a student. These were consistently a very pleasant encounter. The interviews usually began with a short recap of the situation over the past twenty plus years that we hadn't seen each other; in the interview itself we could refer back to shared prior experiences and specific situations at the school, etc. The interview usually lasted two to three hours with these respondents. With two exceptions, these respondents chose their homes for the interview place.

The interviews were conducted according to a previously determined script:

1. Which **historical/social events have personally influenced you in your work**? How has society's transformation influenced you (i.e. the development following 1989 compared to how you lived before that)?
2. Have you experienced any **dilemmas in teaching** that were linked with these changing social and political contexts? What were these dilemmas? Examples? (Note: We understand a dilemma as an uncertainty or difficulty in deciding how to act in a certain situation).
3. The social transformation also led to school reform. What are the main changes in your school? Have the goals of education changed at all? What else has changed regarding school culture? Was school reform carried out in line with your expectations? What was **successful and not successful** in this reform – in general and specifically at your school?
4. How did the transformation influence **relations** between students and teachers?
   - How did the transformation influence mutual relations between teachers and between the teachers and principals?
   - How did the transformation influence relations between students?
   - How did the transformation influence relations between teachers and students' parents?
5. How did the social transformation influence **expectations of you as a teacher by colleagues, principals, students and parents?**
6. What would need to change so that you can perform your job as you wish? What would you **need/like/ so that…?**

In all cases I began with a broadly formulated question: "Which social changes influenced you in your work?" In later parts of the research I supplemented this preliminary question by asking what in the teachers' views really changed or did not change.

After this, the interview usually developed according to the subjects the teachers themselves touched on. They were, however, asked all the aforementioned questions. If the respondents gave overly generalized answers, I additionally asked that they recollect a situation that could support their answers (Can you recall specifically something that occurred? What was it like? What is it like when the students are rude to each other? What was it like before? etc.).

Interviews with current teachers at Chestnut School were conducted in the school as requested by the respondents. The interviews generally took place in a small kitchen next to a conference room, while the interview with the principal and vice-principal took place in the principal's office. These interviews were generally shorter, lasting an hour or two, and the teachers were not as willing to talk about their own experiences. They kept strictly to the topic of transformation in education.

At Linden School the interviews were conducted in the opposite order; it wasn't easy to speak with the older generation of respondents in the initial phase. While the current teachers preferred to talk to me at the schools and the interviews were shorter, the older generation preferred speaking to me in their homes and the interviews were much more of a biographical nature.

The interviews were recorded and transcribed, always with the respondents' consent. Analysis of the gathered data was carried out in several phases, predominantly employing the method of Miles and Huberman (1994). First-level coding was composed of previously prepared categories derived from the research questions (historical events, relationships, dilemmas, reform, expectations of a school). In the research this coding was expanded to include the biographical observations of the respondents.

Another step in first-level coding was analysis according to the occurrence of some words indicating causality (such as "because") and turning points.

Patterns coding followed first-level coding. This was mainly geared to the relation between the topic and the explanation of its occurrence. Both of these activities were supplemented by constant notes, records and partial theories. The creation of constant reports preceded the final analyses and results.

In the final phase, the passages of the interviews used in this book were authorized by the individual respondents. Authorization was given over the phone and via e-mail. In two cases, teachers refused to allow use of a specific passage – the former principal of Chestnut School backed away from her testimony and at the last moment distanced herself from it. The second instance concerned a current teacher at Chestnut School, who justified her decision by rejecting the grammatical level of the still unedited rewritten text. Yet not even after it was properly edited did she give her consent to the use of the passage.

Respondents allowed the use of authorized passages on the condition that they could grammatically correct them. They felt that it would be shameful if their ideas were conveyed through their vernacular expression. Distinguishing between the written and spoken word was important for the respondents and evidently was related to their idea of how a teacher should express him or herself. The published passages were therefore corrected: 1) I corrected incomprehensible sentences so that their final version was comprehensible upon the first reading. Ambiguity often resulted from the respondents pondering their responses and other comments and then clarifying them. The complete versions of the unaltered text are available in my archive. Nevertheless, the changes never altered the essence of the message, and the words used were not replaced. 2) Non-standard endings typically used when speaking were partially corrected. 3) Vulgarisms or the occurrence of the non-standard words were not changed.

What the respondents didn't say: Reviewing documents

Three types of documents were analyzed as part of the research. One of these consisted of annual reports provided by both schools. It is worth mentioning, however, that schools only have annual reports available for the past ten years. Annual reports from the first years following 1989 are not available, not even from the local museum or district archive. The current principals of the schools don't even know what became of them. These documents are mainly used in the first part of the text – in the description of the examined environment.

Another important source of information was the chronicle of the town of Remízek kept in the local museum. A third source were documents from the district archive in Lán. The main reason I looked through the archive was to try to find out how many students prior to 1989 received evaluations not recommending that they proceed to secondary school. Yet these evaluations could no longer be accessed. According to the staff at the district archive, they were assigned to the "S" (To Be Shredded) category. At least I was able to examine the entries from the chronicles of both schools from the 1980s and the minutes from the teachers meetings for that same period.

Parents and children

As soon as it became apparent from my research that an important subject of present-day schools is relations with parents, I began to consider conducting interviews with them. The way to reach the parents was a little different at each school. At Chestnut School the interview concerning authorization with the teacher Mrs. Krečmerová played a key role. She was curious about the research results and began to ask how I viewed the entire situation. I described to her what all the teachers had said – that they felt that there was a difference in values between themselves and the parent – and that it would obviously be ideal to ask the other side – the parents – how they felt. The teacher herself came up with the idea to have a parent-teacher conference for this purpose. Such meetings are always held in April in the form of a consultation. Waiting in the hall for their turn, the parents would theoretically have time to answer my questions. I then had to have this plan approved by the principal.

When I arrived on the arranged day, it was clear that the other teachers also knew that I was going to speak with the parents. The reception I received in the hallway outside the staffroom was rather affable. A room was reserved for me next to the classroom where consultation with the parents was being held. The teacher Mrs. Krečmerová also spoke to her colleague, who allowed me to introduce myself to the parents in her classroom. In both cases it was the 6th grade. I introduced myself to the parents, asked to interview them and then waited in the adjacent room to see if anyone would show up. Only four parents came to speak with me. Organizing a focus group proved impossible; the parents had no interest in taking part in the research.

At Linden School I first asked the principal if I could also try speaking with the parents. Two class teachers, whom I had interviewed and whose students were in the same years as the students at Chestnut School, were recommended to me. One of them was on an overnight field trip with her class, but the other agreed with the interviews. In her class, the parent-teacher meetings are conducted in the following way: The students and teacher prepare for the parent-teacher meetings the whole afternoon. They bake a cake for the parents, prepare other refreshments, and rearrange the desks and chairs to create a long table in the middle of the room where the parents can sit. The students can also take part in the first part of the parent-teacher meetings since, according to the teacher, nothing is discussed there that the students don't already know themselves. Then the children wait in the hallway where I had a chance to speak to them as well and to ask them to fill out the School Culture Scale.

This arrangement enabled me to conduct a half-hour interview with parents as part of a focus group without the presence of their children and the class teacher. The atmosphere was very relaxed; it was clear that the parents were curious and eager to share how they felt about their relationship with the school. Some twenty parents attended the parent-teacher meetings.

I asked the parents previously chosen sets of questions derived from the interviews I'd already conducted with the teachers. These were the sets:

- What are **your expectations of the school**, with what should it equip your children?
- How does **today's school differ/not differ from the one you yourself attended** as a student?
- Does a **family's social situation** play a role in the kind of relations your child has in the school?
- How does your child spend **his free time**?
- What are the **relations among parents** like? How do you spend your time together or not together outside the school?

Even though this research mainly focuses on the view of teachers, for the sake of providing a complete picture I also needed to work with the children's view: how they feel in school and how they themselves perceive the school culture where they spend a significant part of their day. I therefore used the School Culture Scale developed by Higgins-D'Alessandro – Sadh (1998). This tool is based on the responses of children to a set of questions using the Likert Scale[3]. This was created as part of the broader *Just Community School* project, whose goal is to democratize the school, create a community of children and teachers and the perception of the school as a microcosmic society. This pedagogical concept is derived from Kohlberg psychology (Higgins-D'Alessandro – Sadh, 1998). It is in the very environment where the *Just Community School* concept is applied that there was the need to measure its success. Therefore, a questionnaire monitoring four dimensions was created:

- The degree in which normative expectations exist.
- The quality of relations between students and teachers.

---

3   A five-value scale where respondents choose one of the options from "strongly disagree" to "strongly agree".

- The quality of relations amongst students.
- The degree to which students feel that the school is preparing them for further educational opportunities.

In the case of the original research, Higgins and Sadha used the questionnaire as the primary method for examining school culture in a given environment. Essentially all students and teachers filled out the questionnaire and the data could be assessed quantitatively. For this research the questionnaire was only used in the classes of students whose parents took part in the interviews. It is therefore more of a probe into the atmosphere of one specific class.

Yet over the course of the research it proved to be a tool that could be even more broadly applied in assessing the environment at various schools in the Czech Republic. It could thus be used as a tool for schools to evaluate themselves. Not only could a school be described based on the results, but it would be possible to detect weaknesses and develop a strategy to improve the overall environment of schools. The original School Culture Scale was also used for this purpose.

The researcher as a former student

That the book is partially based on interviews with my former teachers is a point that has already been explained. Since, however, in doing so I enter into the story itself, I need to examine in greater detail my relationship to the explored environment.

I consider it an important factor that I had not had personal contact with the teachers at the schools in my research for over twenty years. Neither had I maintained contact with any of my former classmates, nor with the people of the town of Remízek. I would even say that, from a present-day perspective, I am to a certain extent a neutral observer of local events.

Yet this neutrality obviously does not apply with regard to the willingness of the older generation of teachers to talk to me. Some of the teachers at both schools remembered me. It was clear in all cases that this greatly enhanced their willingness to trust me.

The fact that some teachers remembered me positively affected the course of the research. Never did I feel that the teachers wanted to hide something from me. The ability to relate to certain situations well known to the locals then facilitated communication. Upon realizing that I was well informed about the local area, they were willing to go into greater detail in the interviews.

To acquire the necessary distance, I chose a method of self-reflection that I supported by keeping a thorough field journal. I was aware, however, that my view of both schools was partially distorted by the fact that I had experienced one 'from within' as a student, but not the other. I was hit by a *déjà vu* sensation when I arrived at Chestnut School for the first interview, and heard from the first two or three respondents the same sentence: "Nothing has changed here over the past twenty years," which my visual perceptions confirmed. The school really looked the same, including the color of the hallways outside the staffroom and principal's office. In the hallway I encountered my former chemistry teacher who was carrying the same bag I remembered him having twenty years ago. We both shared a laugh when I pointed that out. It was for this reason that I began to systematically ask the teachers what in their view had changed and what hadn't.

A thorough categorization of the individual interviews during the research assessment provided me with sufficient distance from my perspective. Nevertheless, I feel that the method I chose of interviewing in their 'own' environment has its limits. If my contact with this environment had been more intense and the research results could influence my current structure of relationships, this proximity to the examined environment would already be to the detriment of the research as such.

Since, however, I have from today's perspective no reason to conceal the research and its publication cannot in anyway negatively influence my current relationships, I feel that the method I opted for was the only way to research a subject that is as intimate as the transformation of a culture in a specific – to a certain extent closed – environment.

3. About Remízek and its milieu

The town of Remízek

The town of Remízek lies in Central Bohemia about an hour's drive from Prague. To a certain extent, this defines the parents of the children from both examined schools – many of them commute to work in Prague.

Remízek is a town with pleasant natural recreational areas. There are some 10,000 inhabitants in the town. There are two basic schools, one training school, a vocational school and several nursery schools.

The town runs a local library and museum. A few non-profit organizations are located in the town and churches have strong footholds: both the Catholic and Protestant parishes are active cornerstones of the community. An aristocratic chateau is one of the town's dominant features.

According to the election ballots for 2010, eleven political parties were active in Remízek. All major parties were represented here including the Civic Democrats (ODS), the Czech Social Democrats (ČSSD), Public Affairs (Věci veřejné), Top 09, the Czech Communist Party (KSČM), the Citizens' Rights Party (Zemanovci), the Green Party and the Jana Bobošíková Free Party. There are also a number of local groups in the town. The town hall was politically controlled by a coalition of Civic Democrats and Social Democrats.

The ballots for 2010 shows that none of the current teachers or principals from either schools ran for election in the local elections. The town's mayor and deputy mayor serves as the link between the schools and the current town hall. The mayor, Roman Zámečník, had actually become principal of Linden School in 1993, while the deputy mayor, Monika Kelerová, was a tutor at Chestnut School.

The chronicle states that the Civic Forum (the political platform founded by Václav Havel and his colleagues in 1989 that became a catalyst for political changes in 1989 and the years to follow) had already been established in the town in November 1989. In fact, Monika Kelerová, who became one of the first spokespeople, played an important role in establishing the Civic Forum in Remízek. She was working at that time as a tutor at Chestnut School and took part in the changes at the school. We also know from the chronicle that many townspeople joined the Civic Forum, which mainly organized round-table discussions where thorny questions of coexistence were dealt with and suggestions were made for changes that arose from the new social and political situation. The Remízek chronicle indicates that 26 February 1990 is a triumphant date since the OF candidates were successfully added to the Town's National Committee even before the first free elections.

Nevertheless, in the early post-revolutionary years the chronicle's entries are paradoxically very brief; it wasn't until after 1995 when a new chronicle was started that the descriptions of town life returned to their original length. From that point until now the chronicle demonstrates great continuity; its detailed records of life in the town, just like the relatively extensive museum, provide sufficient information on local events.

The stories of the Chestnut and Linden schools

I began my research in the spring of 2010 by interviewing the older generation of teachers at **Chestnut** School. However, it soon became apparent from various remarks that the lives of the teachers at Chestnut School are strongly linked to those at nearby Linden School, and that the research would need to include both schools.

Remízek has a long tradition of education. The first school was opened in 1774 with classes taught in three rooms in a family house. The creation of the Linden School dates to about a hundred years later and was inaugurated in 1899. At the time, this was the only school in Remízek that met the capacity demands of that period. The situation changed in the 1960s when Remízek and its environs became more industrialized, which led to a wave of new working-age inhabitants. Some teachers recall that the situation was already critical before the new school (Chestnut) was opened. The youngest students at Linden School were taught in shifts, in pubs, at the pharmacy, anywhere there were available rooms.

It was thus a great relief in 1964 when Chestnut School opened. Chestnut was built right next to Linden, practically on the same parcel of land. Yet visually the schools are very different. While Linden School is an old, multi-floor building, Chestnut School is built from prefabricated panels.

The opening of Chestnut School was obviously accompanied by the movement of teachers. Much of the Chestnut staff consisted of teachers from Linden. Teacher transfers were linked to the principals in charge who chose their subordinates upon agreement. This division probably took place without major problems – the teachers decided amongst themselves who was going to teach where. I didn't detect any friction regarding this situation in any of my interviews with the teachers from both schools. Instead, everyone remembers feeling relieved by the division of the schools. The headcount in the classrooms was reduced, organization was streamlined, teachers suddenly found themselves in a group that was better arranged since it was smaller and the staffroom was once again large enough to enable the teachers to gather and normally communicate.

Teachers from both schools remained in contact with each other. Nevertheless, at both schools the prevailing view is that relationships were better prior to 1989 and that the people at both schools were closer to each other, which was evident in a broad range of social events, trips, etc. When comparing the two schools in the teachers' recollections, Linden is seen in a more positive light than Chestnut. The teachers at Linden would gather every Thursday at a pub. There was no obligation; they had a table reserved and whoever felt like coming could join in. The teachers from Chestnut – those considered the "core" – would join their colleagues from Linden since "they had more fun there". According to teachers from Linden, even the International Day of Women and other regular events were celebrated with the teachers from Chestnut coming to Linden.

The year 1989 brought about a fundamental change in the relations of the two schools. Although in both cases relations were destroyed, at each school this destruction followed a different script, took place at a different time and politics played a different role. We will return to the essence of this destruction later.

The situation at Linden was unique in that fundamental changes at the school had only begun with the competition for teaching posts in 1991. The principal, Mrs. Zemánková, who had worked at the school since 1965, remained as principal until the competition for all positions was announced. She also took part in the competition in an attempt to retain her position. However, the commission chose Mr. Zámečník, a young PE instructor from a school in the Lán district, to head the school. After he took over, a protracted conflict ensued that resulted in nearly half of the teaching staff leaving. Mr. Zámečník himself left the school in 2000. Following his departure, the school was led by a temporary replacement until a competition was announced in 2001. The current principal, Mr. Řehák, won this competition.

The situation in 1989 at Chestnut was influenced by the fact that that a new principal had arrived in September 1989. The previous principal, Mrs. Zavadilová, had retired and was replaced by Mr. Brož, who had taught for many years at the school, with his colleague, the teacher Mrs. Veberová, taking over the position of vice-principal. In order for Mr. Brož to become the principal he had to join the Czechoslovak Communist Party; Mrs. Veberová needed to become a party-screened reserve. This information was provided in interviews by colleagues at the time. After the political changes began, there was much unrest at Chestnut School. All of those involved remember it a little differently, but it is obvious that a dispute broke out at the school that was completely of a political nature as well as politically motivated. The point of contention was whether the principal could be someone who was a member of the communist party. Some claim that the Civic Forum was established at the school, but others say that early attempts at creating the forum did not succeed and that they had to use the existing structure of the Revolutionary Trade Union Movement (ROH). In any case, however, the more revolutionary minded teachers forced Mr. Brož and Mrs. Veberová out under dramatic circumstances – representatives of the individual groups agreed on this solitary point. Mr. Hájek, a former PE teacher, became the principal. According to a number of teachers from both schools this was typical for the entire district – it was the PE teachers who started the revolution in the Lán district. It's worth mentioning that all those involved remained as teachers at Chestnut School, including the principals, Mr. Brož and Mrs. Veberová, who had been forced out (and they are still there).

The newly established leadership was still in charge at Chestnut School when I was conducting my research. According to the information in the town chronicle, Mr. Hájek had to defend his post in 2005 when he was re-elected in the third round of the competition. Yet it was based on this experience that the town council decided that a competition for the principal's post at all schools be held every five years.

Not only did 1989 bring about a change in personnel; the way in which students gained admission was also altered. Prior to 1989, the children in Remízek were divided between the two schools alphabetically: those with family names from A to M attended Chestnut; those with names from N to Z went to Linden. This rule ceased to apply after 1989 and parents could freely choose which school their children would attend. This change obviously resulted in the development of a rivalry between the schools. The precise number of enrolled students from 1989–2000 could not be ascertained at either of the schools. The town chronicle mentions the number of students at the schools for some years, so we know that in the latter half of the 1990s the headcount at Chestnut School, which had 753 students in 1989, grew considerably. By 2008, both schools had a similar number of students – Chestnut 577, Linden 530. Yet compared with 1989, this represented a slight drop in the number of students at Chestnut. This fact is also mentioned in the school's annual report, which discusses the decrease. According to the testimony of some respondents, the administration dealt with this situation by not prolonging the employment contract for roughly one teacher per year.

Linden was always dealing with and continues to deal with a lack of space in the building, which does not fit the school's actual needs. In 2002, the school authorities even requested that the Ministry of Education approve an increase in the school's capacity from 542 to 610 students, which it did.

After 1989, both schools became more specialized. Chestnut focused more on sports activities with the curriculum modified for athletically gifted students. The school excelled in soccer and gymnastics. The town chronicle describes in detail the school's success in various district and national competitions. Oddly, these successes are not emphasized in the available annual reports, nor did the teachers mention them in the interviews.

Following 1989, Linden began to focus more on the humanities and creative activities and was successful in these areas. In 2005/2006, a school club was set up, offering a broad-range of activities. The school took part in numerous trips, performances, retreats, competitions and projects, etc. In 2008, a school board was established with three representatives.

In 2004/2005, the Center for Lán School Services praised the Linden School's active interest in the program for the Further Education of Pedagogical Workers. The clear overview of completed courses is an integral part of all of the school's annual reports. Slightly beside the point but still worth mentioning is that the annual reports of both schools differ: While Linden has quite elaborate annual reports, those of Chestnut are always only two or three pages.

According to the chronicle and annual reports, both schools are open to the community – Linden organizes each year a Christmas mixer for the town, while Chestnut puts on a Christmas market and "fairy-tale forest". Linden School is working with town representatives to assemble a Student Board.

During the research, the town vice-deputy revealed that the situation of the schools in Remízek was being dealt with, that the capacity of the local vocational school was not being sufficiently utilized, and that the town was therefore negotiating with both schools to place more children in the vocational schools. These negotiations ultimately led to the idea that a vocational school be transformed into a primary school geared toward children with learning disabilities. This option is currently being discussed.

Respondents

Several steps were taken in selecting the respondents. Part of the selection was calculated – these were the teachers who had taught at Chestnut around 1989 as well as teachers now teaching there. The snowball method was then used in the individual groups to choose a sample of the respondents. This consisted of me requesting additional contacts and getting recommendations from the individual respondents.

The choice of the sampling of respondents creates in itself a narrative that relates to the analysis of the examined environment and to the results that will be presented later in the book. The individual phases of research and the final choice of both schools are thus a direct probe into the researched environment.

The research began among the 'old guard' of teachers from around 1989 at Chestnut School. I conducted the first interviews with teachers who personally knew me. Even though this was a very complicated topic (participation in communist structures, of teachers in various functions, Communist Party membership, etc.), the interviews were conducted in a very pleasant atmosphere and I felt as if the respondents welcomed the opportunity to talk about these subjects. The interviews were mainly conducted at their homes (though in two cases teachers requested that they be held in a local café). One interview usually lasted two or three hours.

There occurred during the research a qualitative change and minor crisis in contacting teachers presently working at Chestnut School. I first contacted the current teacher representative, who also knew me from my years of attending the school. As she suggested, I wrote a letter addressed to all teachers in which I requested to interview them. As I had agreed with the representative, I sent the letter to each of them and then attempted to call the phones in the staffroom and arrange interviews with them. Yet in doing so I was only able to arrange a few interviews. Much of the time I came up against emotionally charged refusals. One teacher, who had worked at the school since 1989 and was still employed there, refused the request, explaining that she lacked the energy to talk about education in her free time and that she was fed up with it. Another teacher gave a similar refusal and didn't feel like explaining her decision: "I don't want to talk about it and don't even want to talk about why I don't want to talk about it," she angrily screamed over the phone (14 April 2011 entry from my field journal). The younger teachers (except for one), whom the other teachers believed to be the source of the concealed generational conflict at the school, also refused the interview request.

The interwoven aspect of the stories of the Chestnut and Linden schools, given by the proximity of the schools and their staff, as well as by the current interest of the parents in their children studying at one or the other school, was evident in this phase of the research. Although the research originally focused only on Chestnut School, I decided to expand it to include Linden School as well.

I began researching Linden School in April 2011 in a different direction. First, I contacted all teachers presently employed with the school and only then was it possible to speak with the 'old guard'. The reason for this was that I needed the current principal to provide me with contacts to the former teachers.

My reception at the Linden School was much different. The moment that the principal decided to take part in the research I was introduced at a meeting to the entire teaching staff. The teachers themselves arranged with their representative a schedule by which the interviews would be held. The representative always arranged several interviews and provided a peaceful place in the library for them. No interviews were cancelled.

An overview of respondents at Linden School[4]

Name	Age[4]	Period at basic school in Remízek	Teaching qualifications	Chestnut	Linden
Bílá	ca. 60let	From ca. 1993	mathematics, civics		x
Gros-manová	Ca. 55–58 years	From 1982; in 1993 she transferred to a different town near Remízek	Czech language, history		x
Hanzelová	cca 44	From 2008	Japanese studies and Japanese language, international certificate of English langue, pedagogical minimum		x
Hartová	57 years	From 1989	1st level and special education	x	x
Hudečková	cca 40 years	Not ascertained	mathematics		x
Kovářová	cca 48 years	From 1997; presently the vice principal	Mathematics, basic technology		x
Králová	cca 78 years	From 1962	Workshop, physics, math	x	x
Kučerová	cca 39 years	From 2010	1st level, andragogy		x
Okázalová	cca 42 years	From 1993	chemistry		x
Řehák	cca 50	Since 2000, principal at present	geography, Russian language		x
Slavíčková	cca 70 years	From 1976; in 1993 she transferred to a different town near Remízek	history		
Zemánková	cca 69 years	From 1965	Pedagogical institute, qualified to teach physics Chemistry, workshop	x	x

---

4   I was able to determine age by directly asking in the interviews or by estimating based on important events in the respondent's life (e.g. leaving exam, start of university studies, etc.)

In the pleasant atmosphere it was clear that the teachers looked forward to speaking about their work and reflecting upon it through the interviews.

The hardest part was getting the contacts to the 'old guard' from Linden School, which was largely due to the personnel changes that had occurred over the past twenty years at the school. I was ultimately able to get several contacts, which then snowballed into even more. Two teachers at Linden School also refused to take part in the research. One of the cases concerned a currently employed teacher who was in a difficult personal situation and refused due to a lack of time and capacity. The other case was a more substantial reason due to the research itself. The teacher in question stated that it would be too difficult for her "to recollect a period when she did things that she is now ashamed of" (field journal entry from 9 October 2011).

Since the current mayor and deputy mayor of Remízek are former teachers from both schools, I also included them in the research. In their cases, the interviews were held in the town hall on the town square in Remízek.

In the interviews I also asked the teachers why they had chosen that profession. I did so since teachers had often mentioned during the interviews that in their eyes it was not an easy profession. Sixteen of the thirty-one respondents explicitly stated that becoming a teacher had been in the cards for them from early on. They had wanted to be teachers as kids and had never imagined doing anything else. In their youth they had often worked with children, led groups and substituted in primary school, etc. Some respondents said that they had been inspired by teachers in their youth who had become role models for them. Therefore, for most of the respondents being a teacher was more a fulfilment of a mission than the usual choice of profession. Only two respondents stated that they became a teacher by virtue of necessity.

The teachers come from a broad range of **family backgrounds**, both with regard to social status and religion as well as the parents' political affiliation. Some respondents came from families experiencing first hand a certain type of communist oppression, especially in the 1950s – "they took away livelihoods from parents, parents [were] strongly anticommunists, father was a kulak, mother wasn't a party member." etc. Some parents of other teachers, on the other hand, were communist party members, though the respondents were careful to specify when exactly they had joined the party. Some accepted the ideological reasons of their parents, while others – especially respondents from the younger generation – openly stated that their parents had joined the party for the sake of their careers.

The political orientation of parents was only partially reflected in the political views of the teachers. In some cases, they assumed an opposing stance from that of their parents ("parents were against communism, so I decided to be pro-communism"). Some teachers explained their positions in 1989 within the context of their life experiences with communism in which their parents were black-listed for various reasons, including two teachers with parents who had emigrated. Yet such an experience did not necessarily influence specific trajectories of education. In other words, some whose parents fit a certain political profile might have become teachers even if e.g. they openly admitted that they had made use of a certain level of protection or had chosen a field of study in which there had not been many applicants.

I asked the teachers about their **studies.** Although there was no one favored response among teachers, six teachers from Chestnut School openly allowed that communist recommendations had played an important role in their lives and some even admitted that their families had taken advantage of good standing with individuals in the communist party to get into university. Two teachers rejected the idea that their political profile had made any difference before 1989.

I'll tell you how it was. It really was glaringly obvious at the law school. I essentially took the exam in a lecture hall, and there were assistants there who were helping certain people. That was the way it was then. And during the oral exam they asked me which countries the Danube flowed through. That was what they were asking me on my oral exam at the law faculty. And then they asked me if I had worked at the Czechoslovak Socialist Union of Youth (SSM), so I said, yes, in sports, and it was settled. The test to study Czech and art was unbelievable. There were some 200 people and they accepted around twenty-two. That was a packed assembly hall. Then they sent some to study Russian, some to study civics. I could have studied Russian, but I explicitly wanted this. So who is sincere... Math and the sciences, these were a lot more lax; not the humanities.
(Krečmerová, Chestnut School, qualified to teach Czech language and art, today teaches English, 51 years old).

The experiences of teachers at Linden are more diverse. Amongst them were teachers whose relatives had been blacklisted by the party and who had assumed that they would not be allowed to study, though they ultimately were. One respondent had chosen a field that was not overly popular; another felt that the human factor won out in her case – she had befriended the son of a member of a communist neighborhood watch group and that had apparently helped her. Some teachers did not get to study in the field they wanted, but were unable to say to what extent this was influenced by the results of their entry exams or whether political influence had determined it. It can be surmised from the teachers' responses that a certain constellation needed to be in alignment for them to study what they wanted with political favor playing an important role at least for some of them. Some who had made use of political protection also said that they were unsure whether it had even been necessary.

Today's teachers are also dealing with questions of their education. This is due to legislative changes in the requirements for qualifications. At present, this is a pressing topic at Linden School, since teachers not meeting these requirements must leave the school, even if their colleagues value them as superb and experienced teachers. They are being released because they did not formally meet the minimum requirements set for graduating from teachers' colleges. Yet some teachers doubt the quality of the studies at these colleges and do not understand why, for instance, an internationally recognized language teaching certificate does not suffice.

Teachers often contemplate their professional life within the context of the school's activities; some of the respondents even spoke about their "mission statement" – a summary of their experience and ideas of how the school should work. These statements had not been required; the teachers had spontaneously summed up their perceptions of education accumulated through the years. Since I feel that these statements precisely characterized the broad range of approaches, I am giving them in a table providing a generational overview.

Mission statement

'Old guard'	Present-day teachers
A school without discipline is like a mill without water.	Before I was a principal making sure that things get done, now I am a principal making sure that things get created.
What I hear, I forget. What I see, I remember. What I do, I understand.	The best educational instance in a classroom is an argument. [...] The children are learning to argue.
They must learn to read – and above all they must enjoy it.	Life goes on and I'm not going to try to stop it. If reforms come, I won't oppose them. If I want to teach, I will have to sit down and familiarize myself with them.

'Old guard'	Present-day teachers
	Children have one chance in life to go through basic school.

These statements well characterize the range of views on teaching that I examined during my research. In analyzing the interviews, we will get to know how teachers apply their views in practice within the microcosm of the school.

4. Teachers talk about their schools

Teachers' recollections are divided by various important milestones in their careers. The period up until 1989 is marked by their thoughts on relations to communism and its influence on the school's events. The year 1989 plays an absolutely key role. The backdrop suddenly and unexpectedly changed in the middle of the performance (Esteve, 2000). You couldn't close schools, incorporate the social-wide changes and then reopen them. The streets were alive with revolution and the teachers continued their work in schools. The revolution took place there in a kind of minimalist play of relationships.

Teachers see the period following 1989 as a transitional phase when not much changed at first and only later did fundamental changes begin to appear. From 1994 to 2005 it seems that the schools were subject to a kind of free fall. The rise of a new generation of teachers combined with educational reform from 2004 then brought with it a new distinct period addressing the future direction of Czech education.

Since teachers themselves perceive these milestones on their journey through the transforming Czech school, we too will follow their story along an imaginary historical line. We will first take a look at Czech education before 1989, then we will thoroughly examine the events of 1989. After that we will look at teachers' reflections over the past twenty years. While school culture will be an important gauge in this, we will mainly focus on the area of symbols, rituals, relationships, history and personal biographies and shared stories.

We will also follow the fates of teachers at both schools with considerable information being added to their testimonies in many points. Yet it will be clear which school a respondent comes from, and we will see whether respondents from the two schools view the various themes similarly or not. The events of 1989 differed considerably at the two schools and therefore this period will be discussed separately.

The Chestnut and Linden schools before 1989

The situation before 1989 was strongly influenced by the political situation under communism and especially by the "normalization", or hardline communism policy of the 1970s and 80s. In terms of how teachers assess the situation in Remízek compared to that of other towns, it seems that, despite the differences between the individual schools, there was a clear consensus how the political situation ought to be faced. All respondents at both schools essentially agreed that they were not overly politically influenced by the principals of the schools. The principals of both schools – it seems – took the necessary steps to satisfy their superiors, while filtering the demands from above on running a school and providing teachers with a certain autonomy. According to the testimonies of some respondents who had taught at other schools as well, this was by no means the rule of thumb.

When teachers are asked which historical events influenced the schools, they all immediately name 1989 as instrumental. In their view, that was the year that the course of history changed – both the country's and their school's. Yet the teachers also note milestones that occurred before 1989 that directly or indirectly influenced the schools where they now worked.

The 1960s were for teachers studying or beginning to teach at that time a thawing period that they fondly think back to. The year **1968** and especially the ensuing screenings was then all the more shocking for them. It is evident from the responses that there were not many teachers at both schools who joined those protesting the invasion of the Warsaw Pact troops. Anyone attempting a political protest quickly felt its consequences.

> At the time people were signing *2,000 Words* (an open expression of disapproval of the 1968 occupation – author's note). Woe to the person who signed it. I can give a specific example: Jan Kahánek taught here. He was an excellent teacher, a superb colleague, the kids loved him, simply a teacher with a capital T. Nevertheless, he was forced to leave the school because he signed *2,000 Words*. He ended up a driver, an excavator operator. What is interesting, however, is that he liked the school so much that after 1989 he

returned to teaching – at our very school. So this really resonated with us. The screenings that followed in 1970 were the worst. I think at the time the worst was for those people who were in the Czechoslovak Communist Party and didn't like it. That was probably even worse. But as teachers we had to go through it too. What were we supposed to say when asked about 1968? My response to the Central Committee of the Czechoslovak Communist Party was: I was very, very surprised and could not come to terms with it. Really? Then they'd ask what I meant by coming to terms and such. You'd try to gloss over it because you liked working at the school and wanted to stay; so you'd try to gloss over it.

(Mrs. Zemánková, former principal at the Linden School, qualified to teach physics, chemistry, workshops, ca. 69 years)

Several respondents stated that it was clear that whoever was politically involved had to leave. Mr. Kahánek paid for it and had to leave the school. Another respondent remembered a teacher from a nearby village school that met with the same fate. She recalled that the teacher had recorded during 1968 what people said at various meetings in a local pub. The teacher Mr. Brož had signed a petition against the troops' occupation and for the remainder of his life during communism he was blackmailed and forced to make various concessions, to become involved in clubs and even to join the Czechoslovak Communist Party. The then principal at the Linden School told teachers quite openly that they should be glad that they hadn't signed *2,000 Words*, otherwise they would have had to leave.

The consequences of political decisions in the 1960s and 1970s were often borne by the entire family; couples mutually balanced out their activities or political misdemeanors. Another teacher, Mrs. Králová, a member of the communist party since she was 19, remembers how her behavior at the screenings was influenced by her husband's situation:

In 1968 it was a family matter for us since shortly before the troops entered my husband had joined the communist party. Since he had worked in the uranium mines and was an engineer, this was a career move by which he could assume a higher post. And it was expected of him that he would be a party member. And in 1968 my husband protested something, he wrote a letter. And he asked me if he should sign it? I told him that if he wanted to say something and that it's his belief and he knows that it's true, then he should sign it. If you just send it unsigned it's worthless. So he signed it and ended up losing his job. They relegated him to working as an ordinary grunt in the mine and a year later he was forced to leave altogether. He worked for a year in an affiliated machinery plant that repaired parts for the uranium mines. Then a year later they told him they needed him to come back. But he no longer worked here at the mine but at some isolated workplace that he had to commute to. The schools then also underwent screenings but I didn't want to get involved. I held my tongue so that I could at least remain at the school.

(Mrs. Králová, Linden School, qualified to teach physics, math, shop, ca. 78 years of age)

Similarly at Chestnut School, the teacher Mr. Brož accepted his forced involvement in the Czechoslovak Communist Party. Because he had a disabled daughter, his wife, who taught at the same school, was left alone. Nobody forced her to do anything and did not call on her to join the communist party.

Teachers did not enjoy recollecting the screenings and it was clear from their responses that they took part in them and tried to at least save a little face but also not to lose their jobs. "I was surprised and couldn't come to terms with it" – that's how principal Mrs. Zemánková responded to the screening question of what she thought of the occupation of Czechoslovakia by Warsaw Pact Troops. She called this "glossing over" interview questions.

An exception was the teacher Mrs. Slavíčková. She believed that her family was blacklisted – "my father was a kulak, my mother was a dame." During the screenings a parent of one of her students saved her. According to her, the parents knew that, given her family's situation, her history lessons would always be legitimate. Many held her kind approach to student and her curriculum in high regard. When she thinks back on the screenings, she's still amazed that she was able to remain at the school:

I think that the students and parents liked me. So they didn't dare go after me. Then, after the screenings, I had a bit of luck as well. One parent spoke to me. We were talking and he asked me about the *2,000 Words* and I said something and he said he couldn't write that there. And he wrote something there, I can't remember what, they didn't let us read it. I guess somehow it got lost on his desk.

(Mrs. Slavíčková, Linden School, qualified to teach history, ca. 70 years of age)

One other event followed the screenings that was crucial for some teachers in terms of how they viewed themselves as participants of events in society. In 1970, teachers swore their allegiance to the republic – at least that's how it was recalled by Mr. Brož who viewed this act as something that broke him. Mr. Brož was the first of the respondents to recall this vow and recalled that it took place in a prestige hall of a local aristocratic chateau. Upon further questioning, however, most of the respondents do not remember this event or, in other words, it was clear that this was an unpleasant question for them and they were quick to assure that certainly nothing took place in a prestige hall. Only three other respondents recall the vow itself. A local chronicle offers a record of this event.

> A meeting of school principals and school employees was held in Lán at the end of August. It was also attended by teachers of our schools of the 1st and 2nd level. It was declared at the meeting that teachers would raise the youth in the spirit of a scientific worldview, internationalism, friendship to the Soviet Union and of the principles of the moral codex of the builders of communism. They were to strive for unity of school and family and to get parents to join the Association of Parents and Friends of Schools for Political Involvement.
> (Chronicle of the town of Remízek pp. 180–181)

According to the chronicle, the public pledge occurred after 1968 at a meeting of teachers in a district town and not at the aristocratic chateau. The pledge was, however, required of teachers, and teachers most likely performed this duty.

Twenty years of normalization followed the turbulence of 1968, during which, in the teachers' views, things were in a free-fall.

> Nobody left. Everyone stayed there. Yet with such restrictions the group leaders could not perform their role. And I know that ultimately we then continued to teach the children, whose parents did not agree with the approach, and made it known somewhere, or revoked their communist membership. Even those children that I taught got to secondary schools. They took the path of least resistance. They didn't enroll in the grammar school in Lán, but enrolled, for instance, here. So as a teacher I don't remember any great deviation occurring, or that a kid wasn't allowed to study what he wanted.
> (Mrs. Bílá, Linden School, qualified to teach math, civics, ca. 60 years old)

But this free-fall had its rules and the glossing-over between one's convictions and the political dictate was an integral part of life of all teachers. It is worth mentioning that during the interviews the description of the state of the school before 1989 had a different quantitative representation at both schools. The "glossing over" was a very sensitive topic at Chestnut School – many teachers spoke about it and provided more stories and examples. Thanks to these testimonies we can form a quite detailed picture of the political influence on the school and on the relationships between teachers.

The Linden School is different in this regard. The teachers from the older generation agreed that the school principals did a good job filtering the demands from above, and that the teachers mainly taught and had a decent setting for their work. Considerably fewer mentioned the period before 1989 and, if they did, they recalled specific content or other political requirements that they were somehow able to deal with.

I have divided the responses of teachers on the influence of society on the events in the school into several sections in which this influence was obvious and teachers had to deal with a number of quandaries.

What was taught and how

The political system affected schools in several regards. The teachers' daily bread – the teaching itself – was influenced in multiple ways. The curriculum's content was given in advance and teachers were not allowed to introduce additional aspects of the subject covered. Therefore when teaching Czech language, teachers were not allowed to discuss all authors, but only those politically and ideologically acceptable; modern history in the eighth and ninth grades was reduced to an overview of the Czech Communist Party congresses in Czechoslovakia and in the USSR.

> History consisted of two or three little books. I still remember where it was: The tenth congress of the Czechoslovak Communist Party; the tenth congress of the Soviet Union, the eleventh congress of the Czechoslovak Party; the eleventh congress of the Soviet Union. It was horrible, simply horrible. The kids of course couldn't get anything out of it and neither could I, so when they were supposed to be tested they would say something about the tenth congress and then say the same about every congress and would always get it right. That was a horrible textbook. I remember that it was abysmal, simply abysmal. But I guess they had orders from above. I don't know. On the other hand, the kids really didn't have to work hard. It all depended on the teachers; everything really depended on how it was taken.
>
> (Mrs. Veberová, Chestnut School, qualified to teach Russian, Czech, also teaches German, ca. 58 years old).

According to the teachers, the curriculum's content was to be modified ideologically, but also with time allotments. "Two weeks were given for America and half a year for the USSR."

Teachers allegedly were sometimes supposed to introduce into the curriculum false information (e.g. distorted data on biological experiments in the Soviet Union) or extra information on Lenin for anniversary years commemorating the Great October Revolution, as well as on the liberation of Czechoslovakia by the Soviet Union in 1945.

The method of how a subject was to be taught was important for teachers. It was the teachers of the humanities that felt the heavier ideological burden, while mathematicians and teachers of the natural sciences felt that they had it good since "1 + 1 = 2 in any regime."

But math teachers also felt the weight of politics: in 1975 a new concept for teaching math was introduced – the so-called set method. Teachers of both schools remember this as nonsense that they nevertheless had to adhere to. They remember the textbooks arranged so that individual questions were paired with answers that the children and teachers had to learn by heart. Instead of helping, this kind of approach complicated the development of clear mathematical thinking.

Teachers of natural sciences were also obliged to incorporate into the curriculum this educational program and its ideological application. In practice, this meant working out detailed preparations for a course, in which ideological application had to be accounted for as well as objective, teaching aids and methods. The teachers needed to have these preparations worked out for each teaching hour and they were checked by an inspector. Although some math, physics and chemistry teachers may say that they were not affected by this, others recall instances when they couldn't hide behind their subjects.

Believe me, you wouldn't have wanted to be a math teacher. The inspector was always saying, "So, comrade, how is that there's no ideological application. You could have written that the agricultural cooperative produced x square meters of wheat and a yield of x amount of wheat since they used a certain type of fertilizer and had a much greater yield, and this was due to the research conducted by socialist agriculture." Or with the younger students you could count tanks with different military equipment and figure out who has so much of something and what would happen if ... so you've got to include that if there was going to be ideological application.

(Mrs. Bolonová, Chestnut School, qualified to teach natural sciences, workshops, geography, currently retired, ca. 76 years old)

It is also evident that the requirement for thorough preparations changed over the course of communism. While at the start of normalization and, according to all, even before the onset of the Prague Spring these preparations were enforced, at the end of the 1980s nobody had to write them out any longer and inspectors instead checked the classroom performance of teachers.

The teachers were not in agreement on who exactly was the inspector. Most teachers mention the inspection as the main authority for compliance. At the school they felt that the principals did not interfere that much with the curriculum: "nobody really enforced what we could or couldn't teach. As long as nobody complained there was no reason to enforce this." This applied for both of the researched schools. As for the inspectors, a lot depended on the type of person. In the case of the local inspector Mr. Buda, the teachers agreed that, even though he was a pedant, he was an otherwise sensible person whose main concern was that the schools run properly. It was worse when the inspector was from somewhere else. The teachers admitted that they were afraid of such an inspection.

Teachers as officials

It seems that while the teachers were more or less in charge in the classrooms, outside the school there was an elaborate network that strove to make them into "regime officials". The teachers were forced to take part in a broad range of school and extra-curricular obligatory-voluntary activities that were generally delegated to them. Such delegation was not easily rejected, instead they were often accepted due to existential reasons or for fear of consequences. There were a whole range of activities that teachers were required to be involved in.

There were many different **duties** that teachers had to perform for the school. They were responsible for maintaining the bulletin boards that needed to ideologically conform to important communist dates (the anniversary of the liberation from Nazi occupation in 1945 by the Soviet Army, the Great October Revolution, etc.), for the administration of the teachers' offices and for gathering medicinal herbs, etc. Teachers also had to motivate children to take part in lantern marches, in the laying of wreaths to commemorate the liberation and in May Day parades. Extra-curricular activities such as the Pioneer Organization of the Soviet Youth Association, an international communist children's organization in Central and Eastern Europe, also required teacher participation. Civil defense exercises took place several times a year under teacher supervision.

It was in the performance of these duties that teachers also demonstrated the extent of their loyalty, and also, in this case, waged their little private wars.

> The head of the local Pioneer Organization told the children on November 7th: "You will stand there at that monument and you will have only a shirt and a scarf, but no sweater or the like."
>
> And it was so cold, so we tried to stuff the kids in our shirts, but it did little good... So then we got angry because the kids were going to get sick. Those were the kind of events, like lantern marches, we had to take the kids to. There were many such events and anniversaries during the year, and we always had to keep the bulletin board up to date with them. And so we had to teach the children what was on the bulletin boards, who in fact Lenin was. I can still recall that today. Again and again about that Lenin.
>
> (Mrs. Mourková, Chestnut School, qualified to teach the 1st level, currently retired, ca. 76 years old)

Political training and meetings were important tools of indoctrination. It seems as if the obligation to participate in these was in flux over the course of the entire post-World War II period, yet several basic strains of this control mechanism can be observed.

Teachers were obliged to join the Revolutionary Trade Union Movement (ROH) and had to attend its regular meetings. Though it was declared that participation was voluntary, the following story attests to its real voluntary nature:

> I know that there was one colleague who had originally worked at some vocational school and there he fell out of favor due to political reasons and was suspended. They then put him in with us at our school. Well, that colleague really hated to go to the meetings because he lived somewhere in Rybník and had to commute. There was one time when he came to a meeting and I think Mr. Borovička was the chairman. So the chairman looked at his watch, and the principals were there too as they had to be. He looks at his watch and says to my colleague: "It would be good if you could get yourself here on time, comrade. You're five minutes late."
>
> That really angered him; he was such a spirited person. So he asked: "Can I ask a question right at the start?"
>
> "Sure," says Mr. Borovička.

"Are these meetings obligatory, or can they be attended voluntarily?"

Such a question forced the chairman to reiterate the position that ROH was voluntary in observance of teachers' rights.

So Borovička says, "Of course, these meetings are completely voluntary."

My colleague then says, "That's what I wanted to know. Thank you and goodbye." And he grabbed his satchel and went home.

Boy, did he pay for that!

(Mrs. Bolonová, Chestnut School, qualified to teach natural sciences, workshops, geography, currently retired, ca. 76 years old)

Those teachers who were not members of the communist party were obliged to undergo so-called **political training**. According to some teachers, this was by no means merely a formal matter at the end of the 1970s. At the end of the training teachers had to submit and even defend a final paper.

To top it all off, we even had to defend it. That was awful. I can honestly say that we, adult women getting on in years, looked liked the biggest idiots. I was from a nearby school and we had to go to another school to defend our work. And they asked some other questions. I didn't enter into a discussion with them, but another teacher did. It really was horrible for us. I felt so humiliated. I told myself I was too old to defend that baloney. It was bad enough that I had to write it.

(Mrs. Mourková, Chestnut School, qualified to teach the 1st level, currently retired, ca. 76 years old)

Based on the testimonies, less attention was paid to political training at Linden School. Under the supervision of Principal Zemánková, only short meetings were held once a month; the teachers there do not recall this kind of political indoctrination.

The principal, Mrs. Zemánková, and others were obviously communists, but they didn't make a point of showing it. They performed their obligations. We had Monday meetings once a month where some reports were read. We simply had to be there – political training, I guess. So we put in our quarter hour, but those political matters were never overwhelming there.

(Mrs. Grosmanová, Linden School, qualified to teach Czech language, history, currently retired, ca. 56 years old)

According to some respondents, the situation differed from school to school. Some respondents experienced it in the same district in the 1960s and 70s at other workplaces where there was a much stronger focus on political agitation. For all practical purposes, it depended on who was the principal at the school. This applied for Linden School as well. All teachers recall that they were relieved when Mrs. Zemánková became principal. Everyone agreed that in this regard things were very different at the school under the previous principal. Mr. Hampl sat on the advisory committee at Chestnut School and, according to the teachers, his involvement was not overly pleasant.

The topic of membership in the communist party was clearly one of the most sensitive as many respondents were unwilling to speak about it. There were two teachers at both of the examined schools who openly spoke about their communist membership. Others were willing to speak about the membership of their parents or of other family members, but avoided speaking about themselves. These responses enable us to form a picture of how this subject was dealt with in the two schools.

Respondents at Chestnut School agree that most teachers there were not communist party members, though there did exist a small group of party members. This consisted of five or six teachers. Only party members could hold managerial positions in the school; this is attested to by the stories of all principals holding their positions prior to 1989 and their representatives. The teacher Mr. Brož, for instance, was invited to join the party so that he could become the principal. Yet the lingering question is to what extent joining the Czechoslovak Communist Party was voluntary.

The group of teachers who were party members in Remízek immediately fell apart after the Velvet Revolution in 1989; Mr. Brož and the principal, Mrs. Zemánková, recall that they decided to leave the communist party right at the first meeting after November 1989. That they did it in a completely undramatic way leads us to believe that their membership was more a practical matter, motivated either by actual blackmail (in the case of Mr. Brož), by a simple attempt to modify or rectify their standing with the regime, or by the desire to enter a certain profession, even if this meant making concessions to the regime.

The only exception is the teacher Mrs. Králová, who was invited to join the party shortly after being hired for her first job in 1958. At the time, she had viewed it as appreciation for her work and gladly joined the party. However, she too justified this step as improving her career prospects. With the exception of the former principal Mrs. Zavadilová from Chestnut School, none of the respondents expressed any affection for the party and its workings.

One other important bit of information is worth mentioning here: one did not decide on membership in the communist party him or herself, but was invited to join by someone who was already a party member. This happened to several teachers from both schools, who, however, rejected the offer. One of the teachers pointed out in this regard:

> I went through this. Not directly, since I was never in any party and never will be. I don't know why I would... and nobody offered for me to join the party. You didn't just join the communist party, your membership was ordered and only the rarest hero refused it. Refusing membership was really bad. Sometimes people were able to save themselves from it. One of my former colleagues was saved from it by getting pregnant. She was a candidate for membership, so they postponed it, but then the revolution came so she didn't have to. So it was as if she never joined the party. But she had actually wanted to join. There were also those who had wanted to be candidates for membership. They themselves wanted to be, but they weren't approved, so they were very much upset, really regretted not being members, and then after the revolution they were great heroes claiming never to have wanted to join...
>
> (Mrs. Brožová, Chestnut School, qualified to teach Czech language, currently retired, 69 years old)

Another respondent mentioned the direct connection between being involved in the Czechoslovak Communist Party and the possibility of "having a career":

> I'm telling you that I'm the kind of person who never wanted to have a career. I'll tell it how it is. I envisioned more meetings. Yes, the communist members had meetings. I was having a hard time finding the time, since I was a woman; there was a lot of work and I just wanted to focus on my kids. My kids were twelve years apart so that may be why nobody asked me to join since I went on maternity leave when I was thirty-five. And the truth is that she told me, hey, we simply need someone, and I said no, that I will tell her no directly, that I just didn't have the time for it. Then again, if I'm going to be sincere, I can't say that I would have refused on account of ideological differences. I just didn't have an opinion one way or the other. It may sound dumb, but I didn't have anything against them, but then

I didn't agree with them either. It's foolish since a teacher should probably take an interest in politics, but I just didn't.

(Mrs. Rezková, Chestnut School, qualified to teach Czech and French, today teaches part-time, 61 years old).

This generally accepted view, according to which one had to be in the party to hold a position, is in Remízek contradicted by the example of the grammar school there. This grammar school enjoyed for many years a good reputation and, thanks to its principal Mr. Hrabě, was according to many among the more open places, where even people frowned upon by the regime could teach. How did this happen? The principal, Mr. Hrabě never joined the party, and is respected in Remízek as an educated and wise figure. Eva Kelerová recalls that on the occasion of his birthday, when he was already retired, he was invited to the town hall and employees chatted with him. They even dared to ask him whether he was a party member:

He told us a story that at the time Mr. Pazderka was the principal and Mr. Smutný was the vice-principal. Both were screened and members of the communist party. Then his predecessor left the grammar school and was allegedly to be replaced by someone who even terrified those two. He said it in a way that meant that the person was such a party adherent that he was unacceptable even for those two. I don't want to say that he was worse than them, but even they couldn't imagine being with such a person there. So apparently these two tried to think up a way of saving themselves so that they weren't under the supervision of someone so awful and came up with proposing professor Hrabě for this position while promising him that nobody would ever force him to join the party. And sure enough, he said, they kept their promise. It never happened the whole time I was principal. It is true that there were quotas, that for every ten party members there could be one who wasn't a member. He said that he was never forced to join and they left him alone... and moreover they let him develop the school. I was at that grammar school at the time; it really had a high level.

The children of people who had problems in Prague would go to Remízek or to Lán; it was really that good. Dr. Zlatý, who was blacklisted, was allowed to teach here and didn't have to resort to manual labor. Mr. Hrabě made a place for him there. Although he did have to go teach physical education so that he could teach Czech here. But in the normalization period he was fortunate to be able to teach at all.

(Mrs. Kelerová, Chestnut School, qualified to teach pedagogy, currently the deputy mayor of Remízek).

It is apparent from the teachers' testimony that the invitation itself was crucial for joining the Czechoslovak Communist Party or remaining outside the party. If nobody invited the teachers, they didn't have to deal with it. Being invited to join clearly resulted in a crisis that could dictate the future fate of an individual or his or her family. Though teachers were afraid of the possible recourse, none of the respondents mentioned the real danger that would arise from refusing to join the party.

It seems that party membership was not by far the only instrument used to involve teachers in public life. Teachers spoke about it as the **obligatory involvement in public life.** One teacher reflects upon the reasons for this involvement:

> It helped me that I had a high evaluation along ideological lines. Yes, our comrade is working, and she is also doing something for this socialist society, she is trying. That's why others joined the party, to have that "also doing something". Just so that they had peace from such things, that they are not trying to stand out within the framework of the ideology of that time and that they fulfil all educational obligations. A teacher had to be first and foremost an atheist and a Marxist and I don't know what else. The fact that I started doing something was because I was ordered to by the principal: We are setting up a branch of the Czechoslovak-Soviet Friendship Association and you, comrade, will chair it. And it was upon me. [...] That's how it had to be, that's how teachers, like the working intelligentsia, were burdened. The fact that we had to be the working intelligentsia was negatively viewed by society.
>
> (Mrs. Bolonová, Chestnut School; qualified to teach natural sciences, workshops and geography; currently retired, ca. 76 years old)

Public involvement was viewed as a necessary evil, as a way to pay for not being a party member. Since it predominantly concerned women, another decisive factor was how much of a time burden it was, so that it wouldn't overly interfere with domestic duties. There were a wide range of roles offered to teachers. They often mentioned the Czechoslovak-Soviet Friendship Association (the organization of thematic trips, visits from the USSR, thematic bulletin boards on important anniversaries, etc.), the Committee for Civic Affairs (members distributed gifts from the town to those honored, organized the welcoming of new citizens, helped at weddings), two teachers per school were named as deputies to the Municipal National Committee, teachers could become a cultural official for the Revolutionary Trade Union Movement or pass trainer tests. In short, something that would indicate their public activity.

Guidelines often dictated to schools how many teachers had to be named to public positions and how many of them had to be party members and non-party members. It was on this basis that a principal chose specific individuals.

Teachers were nominated to a position by the principal or another head representative from the school. Sometimes it came under a direct threat, other times it sufficed to say:

> Well they were putting pressure on me, this time it was Principal Smutný; he came and said "You have to sign this, you have to sign" or else... They never directly said that if I didn't, they'd fire me. It was more of an existential pressure [...] Instead of in Remízek I would teach at Potok. That's an example. And how would you get there every day with a young child? So you would sign, so that there wouldn't be any problems.
>
> (Mrs. Staňková, Chestnut School; qualified to teach math and art; currently retired and teaching at an art school for children, ca. 73 years of age)

This type of experience was only mentioned by respondents from Chestnut School; according to the testimony, these blackmailing tactics did not occur at Linden School.

In some cases, teachers recalled their participation in organizations in which the performance of their duties was downright humiliating, such as membership in the People's Inspection Committee (VLK):

> A shop was state-owned, but there were sales assistances and managers and the inspection served to make sure that nobody was saving scarce goods for their friends. This is from a time when this was happening with mandarins and bananas. So when we were teaching a teacher with free time would go and stand in line and buy everyone a half kilo of something. It was very unpleasant because when there was a line they would yell, "Why did you give that one so much?" So the teacher would come back and say, girls, I'm sorry, but I only got enough for your kids, so divvy it up somehow. In those days there were a lot of scarce goods that the sales assistants or managers would hide goods under the counter for their friends. But this was happening with everything – clothes, shoes, food. So a supervisory committee was set up that oversaw the socialist distribution to all people, and this was called the People's Inspection Committee – I was a part of it for a few years. Our job was that when there was a lack of goods a message would come from the head of VLK telling us which shops or organizations we were to inspect. So we had to go there and show some ID and that in itself was degrading. I remember going to a shop

and there wasn't any lentil. So we said there isn't any lentil and they said "we haven't been getting lentil. The last time we got some was a few months ago and now there isn't any."

So we said, "can we take a look around" and then they knew what would follow. So we walked around and looked in the drawers. We looked on the shelves and boxes concealed in the corner and found packs and packs of lentil hidden for friends. So then we had to write up the poor guy, he was upset and sniffling and we were repulsed by having to do it, but we were forced to make the inspection. We always went with a supervisor from the district; it wasn't that we went to another town and made an inspection by ourselves. We always had a supervisor with us so we had to make the inspection.

(Mrs. Bolonová, Chestnut School; qualified to teach natural sciences, workshops and geography; currently retired, ca. 76 years old)

Yet participation in the People's Inspection Committee could be of a different nature as well. Mrs. Slavíčková from Linden School recalls that she was responsible for the inventory of illegal goods. This was fine with her since she was against their existence and could at least be useful in some way. It seems from the testimony that the degree of internal resistance depended on how much the performance of the duty was linked to activities that were in contradiction with the teachers' personal convictions, and less so if it was required by someone from the communist authorities or not.

Respondents from Linden School mentioned one event in which they stood up to the regime, under the leadership of the principal Mrs. Zemánková. This was the signing of the so-called Znojmo Call, in which the school was meant to send a few children to a military school. The teachers adamantly opposed signing this.

Mrs. Zemánková was the kind of person that if we said no, then she said no, even if she knew that it would ruffle feathers of party members. So we ended up being one of few schools, maybe two or three in the country, that did not join this call. Everyone else signed it.

(Mrs. Grosmanová, Linden School; qualified to teach Czech language and history; currently retired, ca. 56 years old)

This begs the question of what internally motivated teachers to accept political requests. Another question is what the teachers went through and how they themselves viewed these situations. Some teachers give existential reasons as clear motivation. In their view, it was important to keep their job and regular income, to ensure standard conditions for their domestic life. In addition to this, however, a vast majority of teachers at Chestnut School give as their primary motivation a desire to work with children. Respondents repeatedly mentioned that they enjoy their work, want to spend time with children and make sure that they learn something. Participation in communist structures then represented for them a necessary evil that enabled them to perform their job. "The times were such," "the times required it, "there was no way around it," so they tried to do their job as best they could within the framework of these conditions.

This makes the testimonies of teachers from Linden, who did not actually experience similar dilemmas, all the more interesting. The question then is to what extent were the times really such, or to what extent it depended on how much a given school and its staff were open to the dictate from above. Or better yet, to what extent the school's leadership was willing and able to filter the political requirements and to what extent the teachers had to deal with them themselves without recourse.

Teachers as assessed assessors

A specific inspection tool by the state consisted of the **assessments** that teachers made. They were forced to write assessments of both the children and themselves.

Assessments were tickets to a higher level of the education system and thus a tool of manipulation. They were always written by a class teacher in the final year of basic school for all of "their" children. They were then processed by the principal and approved as part of a ritualized process before a commission.

> The school principal, an official representative, you as the class teacher and perhaps even a communist party representative met in a room. I'm not sure about the communist representative, but it was probably so since they had to know everything best. Then you would take each assessment and read it. They would then nod, yes, and you would take another. Then the parents would be summoned and the assessments were read to them. I know that some teachers had to deal with disgruntled parents, though I didn't. They were always like "yes, yes, nicely written." I never had any problem with that. Because I never wrote there any bullshit, why would I?
>
> (Mrs. Brožová, Chestnut School; qualified to teach Czech language; currently retired, 69 years old)

Different teachers spoke about various parts of the assessment contents. We can derive from the recollections that there was a push for the involvement of children in school and extra-curricular activities – membership in the Pioneers, work organized by both the school and voluntary, trips to visit churches and the involvement of parents. One's background was important – working-class, farming or working intelligentsia. Lastly, the membership of parents or someone else from the family in the communist party was crucial. This point became especially sensitive after 1968 when the entry "is party member/is not party member" was augmented by "was in party, but is no longer."

Teachers recollect assessment writing as an undesirable task; most said that they had to write them and that they tried not to make matters worse for children. Sometimes the teachers omitted to include known information concerning the student and even had the assessment returned to them by the principal (if, for instance, they had not written that the parents were no longer in the Communist Party and "it was known", or that the family attends church).

During the research it took a long time to ascertain how many children received negative assessments and to what extent these assessments could influence the children's actual chances of continuing their studies. The teachers at Chestnut kept speaking about their attempts to write the assessments so as not to hinder the children.

The teachers at Linden spoke about something more. They felt that the parents of children with some kind of political tarnish chose the path of least resistance. In practice, this meant that if a child wanted to study at a grammar school, the parents looked for a school where there was a good chance the student would be accepted. So, for instance, instead of the grammar school in Remízek they would choose a grammar school in a different town. For example, the teacher Mrs. Bílá does not recall that everyone was accepted by the school that they wanted to go to, except for two instances which other teachers from Linden also remember.

Mrs. Slavíčková had a student in her class whose father was a kulak, an independent and comparably affluent farmer targeted by the regime, so the teacher tried to omit this information. However, the school principal forced her to add it in her assessment. Mrs. Králová recalls another case:

> I'll tell you another instance. There was a girl in my class who was an excellent student, very smart and nice, and she applied to a building trade

school. I wrote up her assessment as her class teacher with the help of other teachers who taught there and knew her. But the actual recommendation, the final word, was written by the principal. The principal didn't want to recommend her and so I was trying to find out why since it wasn't fair. And he said, "I know, I'm really sorry, but what can I do?" I guess there was some pressure placed on him. So he told me, "If you want to get involved, go to the communist party's district committee and deal with it. So I went. There was some chairwoman or director of the department there. She listened to me and said: I think you're right. I would sign it, but it's out of our hands. So I asked who I should talk to. She told me to wait, that she would explain it and if they wanted to speak with me then I could go there. So she called the agricultural department. She explained the situation to that person, I have no idea who it was. And I heard how that person was yelling, that no way would our student be going to that school. So I did a little snooping around and found out that she was the daughter of a farmer from Rybník. And that the entire village was against him. Apparently, he had always been an unpleasant person, and that when he ultimately had to join the cooperative under certain circumstances, he decided to have the last laugh and denounced everyone of something, argued with everyone and was extremely unpleasant. I spoke with him only once and don't even remember what kind of discussion it was. They were all simply against him in that town. I know that it was in 1968 that they stood up against him because he made a real scene, pounding the table, breaking a chair, threatening that he'd make them chew up the asphalt on the road that they'd made across his property. So it was more a case of personal relations than political ones. Actually, he had two daughters. The older one went directly from basic school to working as a draughtswoman. A year later the company she was working for recommended her for further studies. The parents chose the same path for my student, Kateřina. She also worked for a year as a draughtswoman. At that point nobody cares where you're from. If the company recommends you, you get into the school.

(Mrs. Králová, Linden School; qualified to teach physics, math and shop; ca. 78 years of age)

A certain denial of the whole situation is evident in Mrs. Králová's testimony: She tried to help a student whose father was probably an ill-mannered person and believes the reasons the student was not accepted was more personal than political. Moreover, she also relativizes the extent the child was affected – she got to study anyway. But it is clear from the responses that this was at the very least an event at Linden School that was more a deviation from the school's usual course.

To understand how much the assessments influenced the children's actual chances to continue studying we would need additional materials – ideally the complete assessments. Unfortunately, these could not be obtained. Yet the district archive provided information that the assessments were filed in the "S" category (= shredding) and that they are no longer available because they no longer exist.

At least the chronicles of both schools and notes from the teacher meetings could be used as secondary sources of information. However, I could not find out the precise number of negative assessments in which it was not recommended that students continue their studies. We know that each year at the end of the 1980s there were a few cases in which it was not recommended that the student advance to a secondary school. Yet the reason given in the notes from teacher meetings were poor marks.

These assessments obviously not only influenced the actual chances of the children being accepted for further studies, they also influenced the ongoing relations between teachers and students. Teachers approached the assessments in different ways. One teacher recalls creating a kind of "questionnaire" that she would send via the children to their parents. She would then try to write up the assessments according to their responses. Another teacher recalls a case in which it was known that the child's father had abandoned the family. The father had a bad reputation in the town. Yet the teacher had to include him in the assessment and also needed to ask her student to provide additional information about him. Talking about these matters was extremely unpleasant for both sides. The teacher still recalls this case and is aware that she hurt the student.

It seems the assessment writing led to awkward situations for all sides. According to the teachers, parents often unnaturally attempted to have the teachers write something positive in the assessments. Then again, for the teacher it was better not to know anything, so that they weren't in the position of knowing something and not writing it in the assessment. And some teachers tried to actively influence parents so that they could write something positive in the assessment. The parents and teachers would then actively encourage their children to take part in some event so that they could improve their standing with the party.

The assessment was ongoing and wasn't just about the student's grades but how involved he or she was in the school. It was very similar to how the principals assessed us. This meant whether the student took part in extra-curricular work, in voluntary work, what the student did for the Pioneer Organization, whether he or she attended church, etc. The class teacher had to write this kind of assessment for the duration of the student's attendance – an assessment about the student's success, characteristics intelligence, how they conducted themselves, both the pros and cons. Obviously, every class teacher tried not to write anything bad about students so that their chances at further education or apprenticeships, which were very popular but also very selective, wouldn't be hindered. So it wasn't easy to assess the kid; and then you had to work with the principal, read the assessments, or the principal would take them, read them and then call the teacher and say – comrade, I'm not satisfied with this. You've written this and that about these parents, but we know that the mother goes to church every Sunday and you haven't written anything about that. Then you say – well, I didn't know that, then you had to add it to the assessment and it would count against the student when he or she applied somewhere. The kids had it good when their assessment included that their father or mother was from a working-class background, and slightly worse if the background was farming, except if the father was a working-class father from the agricultural cooperative and not a private farmer. That was still very good. It was very bad if the student came from an intelligentsia family. A child from that kind of family had to really try to get a good assessment from, say, the Pioneers, so that he was assessed for everything extra he did for the school such as volunteering to plant trees, gathering rocks from farming fields and I don't know what else. These extra-curricular activities would improve his status of coming from a white-collar family.

(Mrs. Bolonová, Chestnut School, qualified to teach natural sciences, workshops, geography, currently retired, ca. 76 years old)

Teachers at both schools all said that in writing the assessments their primary objective was not to harm the children. In their recollections, they see themselves as the ones who were more on the children's side, protecting them from the communist regime. It is apparent from the testimonies that teachers viewed the regime coldly. The regime did not represent their true image of the world; it was more about external conditions that the teachers had to accept to a certain extent. During the interviews about the assessments, several teachers mentioned situations in which as children they had witnessed acts of courage by their teachers and this eventually motivated them to stand on the children's side:

It was in the 9th grade in 1969 when we were filling out some questionnaires on history. One of the questions was whether in our family we spoke about

Jan Masaryk's[5] death as a murder or suicide. Being a naive kid, I wrote murder
with a question mark. My teacher, who was splendid, came to our house in the
afternoon and told my parents: "I wrote in the class book that she was absent"
and he threw away the questionnaire. He did so because that was a questionnaire that the school sent somewhere to higher officials. That was after 1968,
when normalization was starting. The teacher certainly showed courage in
doing that. He knew that if he had left it I would have had problems to get
into a grammar school.

(Mrs. Hloušková, current vice-principal at Chestnut School, qualified to
teach geography, ca. 59 years old).

Not only did the teacher write assessments of the students, the principals also wrote assessments of their teachers. Sometimes teachers were
even called on to provide materials for their own assessments. Again it
is apparent that this differed from school to school and that this practice
also changed through the years. In one case a respondent even provided
the materials that she had submitted to the school's principal so that he
could write his assessment of her.

A) performance of suggestions of the most recent assessment:
Each year I took a course on Marxism-Leninism to deepen my knowledge
of Marxism-Leninism by studying select chapters of Marxism-Leninism. In
this part of my self-education I wrote a theoretical work on the application
of a scientific world view in natural history – sixth to the ninth year, and in
geography sixth to the eighth year. I have not engaged in post-graduate studies, but have continued to improve my qualifications by studying scholarly
periodicals.
B) overall political involvement:
I mainly see the application of the conclusions of the 14th Congress of
the Czechoslovak Communist Party in the party's use of its own subjects. In
natural history this means becoming acquainted with general biological laws
and in the appropriate places of the curriculum with the scientific interpretation of the creation of life and with the overall picture of the evolution of
organisms, of the origin and evolution of man. Thus natural history contributes to the formation of the bases of the students' scientific world view, their
atheistic belief, and the detriment of superstitions and prejudices is taught
in specific examples. A scientific world view and atheistic upbringing is also

5   First Czechoslovak Republic politician, son of the President T. G. Masaryk, who was allegedly
     murdered by Soviet secret police in 1948 after the Communist coup.

formed in geography, especially in the curriculum of the 6th grade, e.g. the earth as a cosmic body. The solar system. In all grades this mainly lies in getting to know the results of socialist and capitalist production relations, their influence on the political and economic arrangement of relations between people in the country and on relationships between individual countries. In this way, I am trying to contribute to the communist convictions of students, who should be able and prepared to act in the spirit of these findings and moral principles. In this sense I also carry out other duties entrusted to me: I lecture on the Soviet Union for the public to educate workers in socialist matters.

Bolonová's comments: So you see, a bunch of empty jibber jabber. That's the kind of bullshit we'd have to come up with to pass muster in terms of ideology and for that socialist education. And since the principals didn't know what to write, since they couldn't write the same thing for everyone, they told us to write it ourselves, and then they'd choose something from that and would write their assessment from what we gave them.

It's deprived, you know, but it had to be that way. We'd have to churn out this nonsense and think up which chapter we could count on to exemplify that scientific world view.

(Mrs. Bolonová, Chestnut School; qualified to teach natural sciences, workshops and geography; currently retired, ca. 76 years old)

The same respondent also mentioned that her family belonged to the working intelligentsia category, and that she herself had to try to make amends for that by attending various groups and taking part in extra-curricular activities.

According to the respondents, the assessments were actually intended to show the state and the system that the person assessed was a fully legitimate member of society or that at least the person had the official paper for this.

But once again this begs the question of to what extent this was an individual reflecting upon a unique experience and to what extent we can take these answers to be representative of the experience in general. And yet it is clear that political profile was more important at Chestnut School. Here more respondents were concerned that nobody could "drag out" something on them. The main sense was not to deviate from the given framework and to try to achieve the maximum within it.

Dilemmas or what the teachers would or would not stand up for

The external conditions under which teachers did their job prior to 1989 obviously brought with it numerous dilemmas that the teachers had to deal with. From the beginning of the research it was clear that this should be more than just a rough description of how things played out. Yet it took a while before it became clear how to ask about the teachers' world behind that external backdrop.

A crucial question proved to be whether teachers sometimes – either before or after 1989 – experienced a situation in which they had to do or say something that they didn't agree with and did not believe in. It became clear during the interviews that this was a question that got to the heart of the problem. The teachers were very often taken aback and then pondered the question, saying that it was interesting and that they would need some time to think it over.

After thinking it over, most of the respondents stated that such dilemmas occurred before 1989, even though a few respondents mentioned that the current way of reforming schools is in their view very similar to the formalized, meaningless world before 1989.

In comparing the responses, significant differences are apparent between the respondents at both schools. The teachers at Chestnut went through a wide array of dilemmas. Thanks to their testimony I was able to reconstruct the main areas of the communist regime's influence on life at the school and on the lives of the individual teachers. It therefore seems that teachers at Chestnut more frequently and more intensively experienced situations in which they had to react to the requirements of the political regime at that time.

Teachers at Linden School experienced dilemmas in considerably lesser amount and intensity. It is as if they somehow had better protection from them.

Despite these fundamental differences, we can divide the responses of the teachers at both schools into several groups. Two basic tendencies are apparent in the reactions to this question. A lower number of respondents said that they had never had to deal with dilemmas of this type. Among them were both principals, who more or less agreed with the regime's requirements. Then there were a few individuals who emphasized the apolitical nature of the school and its educational content, and a few other individuals who mentioned above all their unwillingness to conform in matters that were for them morally important.

The second basic reaction was that the teachers were very aware that they were doing things that they did not agree with and that from today's perspective they are ashamed of.

Yet teachers from both of these defined groups also mentioned other experiences that cannot be so easily classified. Even those who felt the school was a place where they could be their true selves recall certain situations that pushed them to their limits. On the other hand, teachers who saw the school more as a manipulative environment waged their own private wars to maintain their own integrity. A basic indicator, by which the teachers made their decisions, was always more the subject or thing that it was about, and not a general principle that could be applied in every situation.

In examining the theme of dilemmas, I created a table that I hoped would help us understand the complexity of life at a school prior to 1989.

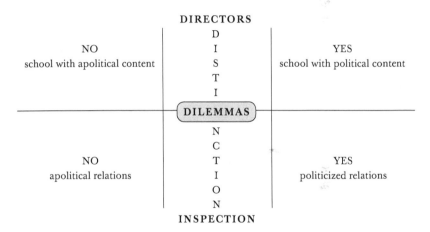

	DIRECTORS	
NO school with apolitical content	D I S T I	YES school with political content
	DILEMMAS	
NO apolitical relations	N C T I O N	YES politicized relations
	INSPECTION	

The former principals of both schools were the only ones who denied facing any dilemmas. The school and the way it was run was for both of them an expression of their worldview.

The former principal of Chestnut was the only respondent who was, even in retrospect it seems, convinced of the ideas of the communist system. Born in 1934, her father supported the ideas of social equality, and from early childhood she automatically took part in activities organized by the Pioneers and Czechoslovak Socialist Youth Union. She sang and danced well, and so naturally joined these activities. Not joining the party was apparently never considered. She does not remember the milestones that lined her political career, such as joining the communist party. Everything in her life flowed almost automatically, including her ascension to the position of principal. She perceived the world then and even today as a place requiring a certain order. It can be better or worse, it can have it deficiencies, but it is always needed. It may happen that a person doesn't like something about this given order or considers something to be unnecessary, but that's just the way it is. This does not mean that order itself is bad. Her basic inner consent with the communist regime formed the setting in which Mrs. Zavadilová normally operated and resolved standard situations, of which some obviously annoyed her. In assessing the situation after 1989, however, she strongly believes that society went the wrong way. She feels that her father, who fought his whole life for social justice, would turn over in his grave if he knew how everything had turned out.

The former principal of Linden viewed the situation prior to 1989 in similar terms. Yet she thought a lot less about the regime as such, but repeated mentioned professionalism that is needed in education regardless of the political situation at the time. She emphasized that none of her subordinates were forced to do anything. For her it was about the school having order. She did not question the regime before 1989. In her view, the most important thing in education is being professional and doing a good job. She agrees with the other teachers that the political theme was not in any way forced at the school. What was important was professionalism under the given condition, which nobody questioned. Everyone agreed that Principal Zemánková created sufficient space for the other teachers so that they could teach by their convictions.

Other teachers agree that they viewed the celebrations of various political anniversaries, speeches and other representative displays as a disruptive element, an unpleasant matter that often caused dilemmas. But it was clear in advance that participation was mandatory, and so they suffered them as the price they had to pay for working with children. These external conditions did not themselves result in dilemmas.

The teachers were much more sensitive in their responses concerning the **content of the curriculum** in their own lessons. Speaking of when they were alone with the children in the classroom was very personal for them. It is clear from the interviews that in these situations the teachers tried to save face and find a certain authenticity in front of the children. Probably since satisfying this inner imperative for integrity and authenticity was difficult under certain conditions, some of the teachers held the view that school should be apolitical, and thus the curriculum should also be apolitical. In their view, a teacher should pass over a certain amount of information; moreover, in the sciences there is less of a chance to influence this content. These teachers feel that there is a distinct border between information that they pass on, and their personal attitude, which does not belong in the class. These teachers probably did not experience dilemmas in the contents of the curriculum.

Math teachers gave one exceptional situation when the government changed in the 1980s the way of teaching math on the first level. It required that teachers use the set approach, which the teachers did not really believe in. According to the respondents, this method consisted of a different way of handling numbers; instead of adding and subtracting, children had to think in categories of sets. The obligatory methods thus meant memorizing whole examples by heart. The material confused the children and did not teach them how to think logically. At this moment, even those who normally would not have experienced the dilemmas came into conflict with the regime. This requirement went against their teaching instincts. The math teachers remember carrying secretly created handouts so that they could make the strict set model easier for the kids. It should be pointed out, however, that this was not an ideological matter, and it was easier at the time to oppose the requirement from above than to go around it.

Other teachers also perceived dilemmas concerning curriculum content. In some situations they decided not to give in. And so they also did not experience the dilemmas, though for a different reason. They set a certain boundary which they did not want to cross in teaching. These teachers obviously had to conform in cases such as overseeing the bulletin boards, participating in celebrations, meetings and other activities. Yet they tried to save face when teaching the children.

No way. Not even during communism. Either I didn't speak about it. I simply avoided it. But I remember that I was very bold before the revolution, when there was an article on the Agriculture Cooperative in the reader and it was distorted in such a romantic way. So I said in a kind of half whisper – children, if you found in Moscow a butcher shop – you probably won't find one, but if you did, a cow would be lying there and that cow would be cut into such thin strips, and whichever strip would be left for you, you'd take. [Laughter.] I told myself that they would take me away. I told myself they'd take me away right away. But under communism and even now I've shared such nice moments with the kids in the class. I don't overdo it, but I never lie.

(Mrs. Poláková, Chestnut School, qualified to teach Russian, music, today teaches English, ca. 45 years old).

Teachers experienced other dilemmas in their **relations** both with the children and amongst themselves. Teachers often tried to behave so that they could save face, and they employed a wide range of strategies to do so. For instance, they would introduce controversial topics when explaining something during a lesson, mention forbidden writers or, against the backdrop of the prescribed material, try to impress upon the children values that they felt were important:

> We tried to ensure that the children were educated and well raised. Of course, when there was history or civics, the politics was squeezed into it, but in a humane way. I remember that when I was teaching the Soviet Union and how they liberated us, my neighbor was General Ovečka, so I had it firsthand. Then someone from the class commented on how the Russians were drunk. And I said that he should put himself in the soldier's situation. For so many years he didn't do anything other than live in the trenches, shoot and kill. And yet he's just an eighteen-year-old boy who wants to dance, love, have fun and joy from life. And they throw him into that situation. And that young person isn't able to cope with it. So you shouldn't be surprised. He looked at me and I told him to imagine that if it were happening now. How would you act? So I tried to explain it to them in human terms.
>
> (Mrs. Slavíčková, Linden School, qualified to teach history, ca. 70 years of age)

In these decisions, an important role was played not only by the teachers' convictions, but also by the actual situation in which they were in a specific class. The children of parents who were strongly in favor of the communist regime could be sitting in the classes. This obviously represented a potential conflict and ensuing problem for the teacher. In such a case, a crucial role was played by the principal, but only if teachers could rely on him or her.

At Linden School, the teachers were supported by their principal. When after one history class a parent of a student came to complain that "comrade teacher" was apparently giving the kids false information, Principal Zemánková stood up for the teacher Mrs. Slavíčková and defended her by saying that the child certainly misunderstood and that she vouches for the teacher. If teachers did not experience this kind of support, the resolve to have courage was obviously more complex.

Yet sometimes teachers within the constellation of a given class could experience the opposite situation. For instance, Mrs. Slavíčková remembers that she once had a class full of children from families whose parents were pressured into joining the United Agricultural Cooperative (JZD), and in that class she was supposed to talk about how it was formed voluntarily.

> Try telling them that the collective farming Agricultural Cooperative was formed voluntarily when half of your class is made up of farmers. But I couldn't just skip over it. So I just covered it marginally, that they were formed and this and that, and read it yourselves. And I talked about something else and distanced myself from it. I didn't want to lie to them at all. The kids ultimately appreciated that as well. They'd say, "Mrs. Slavíčková, you weren't afraid."
>
> (Mrs. Slavíčková, Linden School, qualified to teach history, ca. 70 years of age)

Sometimes the teachers waged their small private wars with the political requirements, and recalled during the interviews with a dose of humor their minor successes, even feeling that they had managed to outwit the regime a little.

> I remember that once during the communist years about twelve teachers came and were to show model classes. I used in mine a spiritual song based on the motifs of Noah's Ark, divided into blocks. I ended up winning the contest and even got a pay bonus for it, but we had to write in the records that the lesson wasn't intended to promote Biblical motifs. There was quite a write-up about it and I had to sign it.
>
> (Mrs. Poláková, Chestnut School, qualified to teach Russian, music, today teaches English, ca. 45 years old).

Even such victories over the regime is then accompanied by an offering to the communist gods – We sang a song with "forbidden" motifs, but we didn't mean anything bad by it.

The respondents often realized that they had got themselves into situations in which they would have liked to have behaved differently and when they even had to act against their convictions. Yet, given the circumstances, in their view there were many reasons why they decided to go along with the situation. This may have concerned the aforementioned curriculum content, participation in extra-curricular activities, the celebration of communist-respected anniversaries, etc.

The teachers mentioned a kind of parallel thought world that they created: "It was always possible to do that so that they were satisfied and it didn't have that effect." To decide how to behave in a given situation, it was important to know whether it concerned relationships or was merely an externally formal demonstration. In the case of a formal demonstration of certain activities, the teachers were much less sensitive – they mostly accepted the given conditions and conducted themselves according to the motto "the paper can bear it." They were much more sensitive in situations in which it concerned specific students who could be influenced or even damaged by their behavior.

The assessments were especially problematic. In this point, all the teachers agreed that they would always try not to harm the children. They saw the assessments as the main instrument or, better yet, the necessary minimum that was part of their professional honor – not to hurt the children. The teachers were willing to make certain concessions so that they wouldn't have to write anything bad about the children.

> Take those assessments. I simply said that I wouldn't write anything negative about the children. For one reason, nobody would read it, except the parents and children. Everyone would get into the school and I couldn't see any reason to write it. I always said that the kids were at an age when they could change a lot. Kids are going to secondary school and already feel like adults. It's a transformative age. So I said that I wouldn't write anything negative. Even if the kid aggravated me. So I didn't write anything negative. I wrote that he was good, even if he wasn't. I didn't write anything that wasn't true, but some things I didn't reveal.
>
> (Mrs. Grosmanová, Linden School; qualified to teach Czech language and history; currently retired, ca. 56 years old)

Yet the teachers also agreed that in various situations they had to carefully determine when to adapt their behavior and when to try to preserve their authenticity. The individual teachers also differed in the extent they considered a situation to be a necessary evil that didn't bother them, and in the extent this dilemma afflicted and stressed them.

> Yes. It was just like that. And I think that there were more of us like that. More of us like that in the school, but we had to say that to stay calm since there were inspectors over us, and those inspectors, well the young kids were afraid that they would go after them. They didn't realize that they were going after us. So if we wanted to stay, we had to say that. We had to say things we did not agree with. You know that there were teachers who sometimes said what

they really thought, and if they weren't found out, then they weren't found out. But if they were, there was hell to pay.

(Mrs. Mourková, Chestnut School; qualified to teach 1st level; currently retired, ca. 76 years old)

One specific situation closely related to the dilemmas was the **inspection**. Teachers partly recalled being afraid of the inspection and were aware that the inspection was mainly aimed at them, not at what the children learned. Experiences with various inspectors were also diverse.

In Remízek, the teachers had experiences with several inspectors; some were worse than others. If, however, the local inspector, Mr. Buda, paid a visit to the schools, some of the respondents admitted that he was examining the professionalism of the lessons and not inspecting the political zeal. Some respondents saw him as a sensible man.

Yet this conciliation with the figure of the inspector did not protect the teachers from specific dramas that clearly show how the teachers mutually worked. For instance, Mrs. Slavíčková was renowned for her approach to teaching history. She described her style as talking to the children. She would sit on the first desk and talk. Obviously when the inspection was made, everything had to be done differently:

One time, they caught me red-handed. Some regional inspector came to check up on my history class. I know that the woman was high up in the ranks. I was supposed to be teaching the workers' movement that day. The inspection wasn't announced in advance, and I wasn't even expecting to teach that at all. What could I do? I had to start. The fact is that our school had excellent teachers. I entered the teacher's room and said that they're coming for me. Brezhnev had just died, so look, here you have papers. Take Brezhnev to class. One teacher lent me this, another that. So I went. Let me tell you, not that I want to boast, but there were tears running down Mrs. Zemánková's face because I had really touched her. [She laughs.] He was near ecstasy, the kids were looking on, probably saying amongst themselves – Mrs. Slavíčková is on her game today, but they didn't play it up. So I said to myself, if he wants to hear it, then he'll hear it. So then I winged it.

(Mrs. Slavíčková, Linden School, approbation history, ca. 70 years of age)

Other teachers recall having problems after an inspector's visit. For example, one respondent had mentioned the existence of the Vatican during the lesson.

The subject of dilemmas also led teachers to talk about their role in society. Are teachers performers of a previously determined role, or are they actors that create this role themselves? The subject of dilemmas was not solely a topic of discussion in the interviews regarding the period before 1989; teachers also feel that there are dilemmas at present and this question should be posed repeatedly with them. In retrospect, Principal Zemánková understands this theme as such:

> I don't know. This country simply ran it this way to meet its goals. And those teachers, since they are disciplined by nature, and if a teacher isn't disciplined, then they can't teach, it simply can't be done. So because they are disciplined, they swallowed their pride, and did it how they wanted them to do it.
>
> (Zemánková, former principal at Linden School; qualified to teach physics and chemistry; shop, ca. 69 years of age)

In comparing both schools in terms of the dilemmas they experienced, we see that teachers from Chestnut talked much more about them. Yet I feel there is a need to mention one situation from the research that is highly significant.

When I requested to speak with the respondents from Linden School, I contacted one teacher highly recommended to me by her older colleague. However, she refused to speak with me, saying that from today's perspective she did not understand how she could have done the things that she was ordered to do. She preferred not to talk since the interview would have forced her to confront her own past. This attests to the depth of dilemmas linked to the overall evaluation of and self-reflection upon one's own history.

In situations causing dilemmas the teachers could not hide behind a previously arranged set of values. Their personal values were often in contradiction with the regime's requirements. And teachers had to act – often spontaneously, without preparing. We can above all reconstruct from today's perspective and from memories whether after these experiences the teachers more felt that they had to do something that they hadn't wanted to do or whether they instead had the feeling that they had managed the situation well enough that they have no reason to be ashamed of it today. In any case it is clear that politics prior to 1989 influenced the acts of teachers mutually – perhaps not always visibly, but all the more intensively.

It is no wonder then that some teachers question in this context whether **politics should be in school** at all. A former Czech teacher says that it always "upset her to drag politics into the school." In her view the Czech textbooks, for instance, were made very well; only the introductions to various chapter were of a political nature. She believes (and several colleagues agree with her) that politics didn't belong in school before or after 1989 – that would solve the problem.

A former Russian teacher added to these present-day associations. She recalled a case in which at one school modern history was taught by a teacher who is still an active member of the Communist Party of Bohemia and Moravia and who teaches history in line with her beliefs, or a teacher who is convinced that the ideal state system for the Czech Republic is a kingdom.

Some teachers recall **political dilemmas in their private lives**. The imperative of a socialist person in some cases directly influenced the way in which they dealt with their religious beliefs or with their choice of partner. If teachers were e.g. religious, they would get into a number of unpleasant situations since it wasn't about what they would teach in school, but to what extent they would subordinate their private life and faith to the external requirements.

In discussing these questions it was clear that the respondents were still afflicted by this influence of politics on their private lives.

At that time they still weren't putting pressure on you to make ideological use of the class, but what they wanted was to work on the teachers so that they took part in all the ideological training by which they were supposed to politically grow, and the most important thing was, for god's sake, not to go to church, which was my case. I enjoyed that and other colleagues did as well. The dear principal was nice to us – "Come on then, comrade, let's have another little talk" – and we would go there one after another and he would torment each of us for one lunch break, saying "comrade, what's your view on it, you yourself understand the sciences, so what's this about a god, you're a highly educated person, what are you doing in a church and why don't you quit going," and I would say that I'm not ready yet, that due to my family I was used to having it written that I belong to the Roman-Catholic Church and that I would leave it at that.

"Well then, comrade, at least think it over,"... and he would keep the pressure on you week after week... And I have to say that even I felt my resolve weakening. I psychologically couldn't take it and went to my hometown presbytery to see what the priest recommended, for even though the persecution was done politely and with a smile, it was still persecution. For the principal it meant being able to report how many teachers he'd converted to atheism, which is why he worked on us. So the priest said that I should go ahead and do it, that it wouldn't be as if I quit the church. My inner beliefs can be completely different from what is written on a piece of paper. So I told the principal on such and such day that I was leaving the church and he was really happy. He sent the report out that he had rid another teacher of an obscure and inaccessible theory and of a poor scientific view. Well it seemed to me that it was even violent of him to try to convince a person in that way that she shouldn't do this or that.

(Mrs. Bolonová, Chestnut School, qualified to teach natural sciences, workshops and geography; currently retired, ca. 76 years old)

It is also clear from the responses that the communist regime was different at this point at the 1950s than it was in the 1970s and 80s. While in the 1950s and 60s it was about the personality of the individual in question – to force him not to go to church, to convince parents not to send their children to church, not to marry in a church, etc., after 1969 what was required was more a formal acceptance of the rules such as celebrating holidays and other communist rituals. It was no longer about the soul, but about not formally deviating. In both cases, however, this *de facto* meant creating a parallel inner world, an inner emigration that created a schizophrenic reality of contradiction between the lived and inner reality. In the case of the teacher, Mrs. Bolonová, this schizophrenia in the example given was even legitimized by the priest, who confirmed the contradiction between the inner and outer world, between the world of personal conviction and that of actual actions.

Two respondents even said that the political reality influenced their choice of partner and later divorce. In one case it was the choice of partner from a working-class background with the belief that one's background does not play a role, which concurred with the official rhetoric of the day. In the second case, a political reason was given by the partner as one of the causes of the divorce.

Even though teachers very much wanted to live apolitical lives, to teach children and to do their jobs well, they had to become political whether they liked it or not since ideology entered their lives through all possible doors. Not because a person could freely decide this way, but because the world was such.

Relations between the teachers

The teachers at both Chestnut and Linden agreed that in comparison with the period after 1989, relations were extremely good at both schools before the political changes.

While the content of the curriculum, symbols and rituals of daily life, just like the dilemmas that the teachers dealt with, were largely influenced by political and ideological events in society, it seems that relations prior to 1989 were nearly apolitical at both schools. Teachers spent much free time together and felt that they had fun in their collective and organized many different festivities together.

Shared history plays a considerable role in comparing relationships at both schools. Some of the teachers originally taught at Linden before Chestnut School was built. One teacher recalls that right before the opening of Chestnut there was much tension in the group of teachers at Linden because everything was undersized. People didn't fit into the teachers' room, there were too many children, great pressure on organizing classes, etc. The situation at Linden settled down when the numbers of teachers and students began to correspond to the building's conditions. Logically the teachers remained in contact with their former colleagues.

A competitive aspect appeared for the first time – the teachers of both schools and their students were suddenly against each other. And since these schools were in a single town, competitiveness to be the best obviously emerged. However, this institutional competitiveness did not damage or worsen relationships between the teachers.

Respondents from Linden said that they were the ones who took the lead in shared activities. Teachers from Chestnut attended celebrations at Linden, since there was always a little tension at Chestnut in comparison with Linden. There were cliques that played against each other there. In comparing relations at both schools, one respondent recalled the moment when the local inspector asked which school she wanted to work for. She didn't know, and the inspector characterized Linden as having a good collective and bad principal, and Chestnut vice-versa.

> That was the competition between those schools. It was a badge of competence; they competed to see who would be better. Our school was a sports school and the other wanted something too, so they established themselves as a math school. That soon foundered since then there was a grammar school and half the class went there. And now on to the olympiad: We were the best

in chemistry, since Zemánková was there. Everyone followed it closely. Some took it a little more seriously; the athletes, Hájek and Neuman. But we would meet as teachers in the pub every Thursday. Both schools. The young teachers. And we'd just talk and have a good time.

(Mrs. Grosmanová, Linden School; qualified to teach Czech language, history; currently retired, ca. 56 years old)

Everyone agrees that there was always a certain contentiousness between some people at Chestnut – "a contentiousness between teachers of the first and second level, between the young and the old." You'll always find people in a collective who break up the overall cohesiveness. That was something they didn't have at Linden, and that seems to be why they could be depended on for the shared activities – the environment here was safer and thus was naturally preferred.

Even though relations at Chestnut appear to be worse when comparing both schools, the teachers said that they were satisfied at the school. They admit knowing who amongst them was in the party and who wasn't, but politics was not discussed at the school, and the teachers could get along normally with each other. Teachers from Chestnut even rate relations in the staffroom and time spent together very highly in light of later events. There "was fun" in the staffroom, they went to play ping-pong and spent breaks together. Some teachers said that though they were closer to some people (usually those teaching in the same department as them), this did not prevent relatively harmonious relations throughout the school.

This also applied at Linden; according to all, there was even less tension here between teachers. Teachers were used to spending free time together and politics did not at all influence relations. Everyone tried to maintain good relations. It's clear that they were able to achieve this, and the teachers perceived the smooth relations as a value in itself.

Well, at our school it was always good. We had a good collective, really good. If someone came to substitute from another town, they'd see how we got along and ask, is this how it always is here? I would say yes. And if young teachers were hired, they'd quickly learn the ropes to be like us, not to envy each other, to help each other. We'd have parties, all together, there was a sincerity to it. That worked up until 1989, then it all shattered.

(Mrs. Slavíčková, Linden School; qualified to teach history; ca. 70 years of age)

Some respondents attribute it to the existence of a common enemy – in the form of the communist regime. Yet it is not clear whether in this regard they are not just repeating commonly used clichés. What is clear is that after 1989 teachers could begin to speak more to the school principal, in which case the common enemy disappeared. Nonetheless, the natural bond of the relations also disappeared, and teachers had to deal with this.

One interesting point was that it was more the inspectors and the external world that brought the penalties. According to the respondents, prior to 1989 principals of both school did not hinder their colleagues in any fundamental way and did not even act as ideology guardians.

While Linden School sailed placidly through the late 1980s to 1989 without being hit by any storms, relations at Chestnut began at that time to reel. Though it is as if the Odehnal case foreshadowed the events of the autumn of 1989, it also nicely symbolized how the relationships at Chestnut were formed. In the spring of 1989, a conflict arose between the school principal and a young teacher named Mr. Odehnal. The dispute even ended up going all the way to the district court in 1989. The goal of this research was not to reveal the true cause of the conflict. Only two respondents even mentioned the case, and this was only in the context of the state of relations at the school. It is clear, however, that even though the faculty's sympathies were divided, everyone took the same car to the district court. They chatted with each other on the way, gave their needed testimony at the court, and then without any sign of antipathy all drove home together: The teachers themselves claim that political affiliation as such did not have any bearing on the quality of the relations at the school.

1989

Mr. Brož – a new principal for Chestnut School

Mr. Brož was born in 1943. Following his studies he was hired as a teacher at a primary school in Palouk where he was working when the fateful year of 1968 arrived. After the invasion of the Warsaw-Pact Troops he became involved and signed a petition against the invasion. He was merely reprimanded for this in Palouk because: "The principal at that time more or less accepted it, so he only reprimanded us." The turning point in his professional life would come later.

> There are plenty who blame us older people for being in the communist party, and yet they have no idea how it worked in education. I think it was the teachers above all who had enormous pressure placed on them. Enormous pressure. That was in 1970. The Russians came in 1968, didn't they, in 1968, and in 1969 there was still some kind of peace shall we say. That was sometime in 1970 or 71. All at once someone remembered that teachers had their hands tied, that a so-called vow was given. And that was in the chateau; all the big shots were there from the district, and from the region, and a representative from the ministry came there. Then every teacher had to sign a paper and swear loyalty to the Czechoslovak Socialist Republic, to the Soviet Union, etc. If someone refused to do so, their career in the school ended that day. No exceptions. I would never even dream that our principal [from Palouk] would then turn, and when I came here [to Remízek] and gave my vow, they suddenly handed me a paper where it was written how I had acted in 1968 following the invasion and that I had signed and that we had demonstrated. So they knew about me and said that if I wanted to teach then I had to join some activity in the city. I had never been involved in anything before, so they forced me to join the civic committee, and then from civic committee they forced me to become a representative, and that's how it went. In short, if I wanted to teach, I had no other choice. I mean, maybe it was a mistake. Someone may hold it against me, but I had my reasons, not political, but family, explicitly family reasons. I had two small young girls, a girl who was seriously ill, and I simply couldn't afford to do something else.
>
> (Mr. Brož, Chestnut School; qualified to teach chemistry, workshops, ca. 67 years old)

Mr. Brož became the principal of Chestnut School in September 1989, when the previous principal retired. After the November revolution, the school's employees did not give him a vote of confidence and he was forced to step down. At the same time he gladly (his words) left the communist party.

> Well, then in 1991 – in fact it was from 1989 or 1990, the teachers began saying that I had been in the party, or that I was in the party and now I'm the principal, and just like everywhere else they started slinging mud and started looking for all kinds of such... The worst was when it came from people with

whom you'd been through everything. I had shared so many different experiences with one colleague, whether it was trips, or skiing courses, theatre, and so much more, and then that year came and I was suddenly the worst person possible since I had been in the communist party. Until then it hadn't bothered him, but all of a sudden it began to.

(Mr. Brož, Chestnut School; qualified to teach chemistry, workshops, ca. 67 years old)

The events of 1989 at Chestnut

While relations at the school were not weighed down by politics prior to 1989, it seem that 1989 impacted and politicized them. When teachers speak of 1989, they speak mainly about relations, as if everything else was of little consequence and from today's perspective was not at all important. For a better idea of what was happening at that time in the school, I will first summarize the sequence of events based on a reconstruction from the teachers' testimonies. We will then interpret what happened to relations.

The situations and events of 1989 were not the objective of my research. The moment that I asked teachers from the older generation about changes in relations, they automatically began mentioning events of 1989. After several interviews it began to be clear that these events were crucial regarding today's perspective of relations at Chestnut School. I therefore deliberately asked the other respondents about them. My questioning shifted from random inquiries to specific questions of what the year 1989 was like at the school and what changes it brought to relations.

It was clear from the teachers' responses that two concurrent events occurred at the school. The principal, Mrs. Zavadilová, reached retirement age and the 'Odehnal case' helped her decide that it was really time to leave the school. In September 1989, a new principal was needed and a teacher, Mr. Brož, was hired. To assume such a position as school principal, a person from the communist party needed to invite him to take over the position. Mr. Brož described this person as a "decent guy". He believes that joining the communist party was merely a formality that enabled him to first become the vice-principal and then the principal.

At the same time, another teacher, Mrs. Veberová, who had returned to the school following her maternity leave, had a favorable communist screening, and thus became vice-principal. In September 1989, a certain destabilization occurred with the change of these leadership positions. Two months later the revolution occurred and with it the political changes. November 17, 1989 was a Friday, and by Monday everyone pretty much knew that anti-communist demonstrations were taking place in Prague, but it still was not clear how the situation would develop. Teachers, however, had to be at school at 8:00 a.m. on Monday morning and begin teaching.

In their classes, teachers were their own masters, independent of their fellow teachers, and they acted that way. Some teachers continued teaching as if nothing was happening ("school should be apolitical"), some discussed what was happening with the students (especially with those in higher grades). Some teachers conducted themselves in class by what was written in the newspapers. Teachers had to deal with a lot more than classes.

The staffroom was filled with tension, even between individual teachers. Some were hopefully anticipating fundamental social changes, others were worried. It was obvious that one couldn't speak with other colleagues about this unusual situation. It seemed as if the revolution wasn't penetrating the staffroom at all. But that was just an illusion.

> No, no, no. It wasn't like that. Not with us, at our school we didn't speak about it. At our school we just accepted it, we just took it how it came. We certainly didn't analyze it openly. It was more like, if that's the way it's going to be, then we'll do it that way and that's that. We really didn't talk much about politics. All of a sudden the gym teachers took it upon themselves and said that we're going to take a vote. And they planned it out, they planned out the school and it was done. [She laughs.] It was in the pub, really; go ahead and ask them, they made their revolution in the pub.
>
> (Mrs. Veberová, Chestnut School; qualified to teach Russian and Czech, also teaches German; ca. 58 years old).

Some teachers said that in those days politics was not discussed in the staffroom; others recall specific critical situations that they discussed with colleagues:

> All at once we started talking about the Velvet Revolution, and it really was quick. I remember that one teacher, whom I won't name, just started screaming at us in the staffroom; she said they'd arrest all of us and so on, that things had to remain how they were; they were threatening that the

communists would hold on, that we only thought that it would collapse. It really did take a week or two before everything crystallized; I know it was like that at the trade school too because I had a friend who taught there. The change was already certain but the communists there tried to keep the truth from getting out, so the discussion in the staffroom was only then reaching your ears.

(Mrs. Zabloudilová, Chestnut School; qualified to teach mathematics; currently a freelancer, ca. 61 years of age)

At any rate it seems that during the first two weeks the teachers tried to figure out which side would win. When it became clear that political changes had come to stay, radical changes were made in management personnel as well, and politics invaded relations in full force.

The recollections of the individual respondents mainly differ in how everything played out. The teachers could not agree on whether a Civic Forum was formally established at the school. Stories also differ on how power was taken over and the old leadership was overthrown. The view of the events is therefore a little foggy. While some teachers said that the Civic Forum was established, and even named the teachers who helped set it up, others (paradoxically the ones named by other teachers) stated that they were unsure whether or not the Civic Forum was run at the school. Monika Kelerová, who was an apparent member of the Civic Forum, cast a light on the situation. According to her, Principal Brož and the vice-principal didn't want to communicate with the strike committee that was set up. Nevertheless, since over a third of the teachers believed there was a need for change in the school's management, teachers agreeing with the revolution decided to join the Revolutionary Trade Union Movement, had themselves elected as representatives and then the principal was forced to communicate with the trade union.

The old leadership (meaning that which had assumed their posts in September 1989) did not survive a vote of confidence. Those involved recall two essential events in connection with this. The former principal, Mr. Brož, and the vice-principal, Mrs. Veberová, remember a meeting at which the revolution symbolically came into being for them.

Then there was a vote on who would be the next representative. Those were very hectic days and I don't really like thinking about it because I still see those people, how we were sitting in that hall, and you're sitting across from them, and this one says this and that one says that against you, and yet I had never done anything to them, and my work spoke for itself. I don't regret it, not at all. I'm glad that I have peace now. The truth is that it wasn't easy to work with those people. [...] Then again, I don't hold it against them. They were so enthusiastic and wanted this enormous change. I guess they wanted it. They simply wanted everything to change. I'm telling you, it wasn't at all pleasant.

(Mrs. Veberová, Chestnut School; qualified to teach Russian and Czech, also teaches German; ca. 58 years old).

Mrs. Kelerová, a teacher, recalled one symbolic event that preceded the meeting. A vote of confidence also had to be made by those on sick leave. Mrs. Kelerová recalled that Principal Brož decided to individually visit the teachers to ascertain their positions:

I recall at that time that those on sick leave were also supposed to vote and that we said that it was proposed to us that the principal would make the rounds and talk to these people. But then we had second thoughts and I went to talk to him and he was acting like... Then again now I can see why. When I went to see him, I told him not to get offended, but that I would like to go with him. That we didn't really trust him. If he were alone with them we couldn't be sure what he would tell them. I don't know if he considered it a low blow that we didn't trust him.

(Mrs. Kelerová, Chestnut School, qualified to teach pedagogy, currently the deputy mayor of Remízek, 56 years old).

Following these events, a competition was announced for the position of principal, which was won by Mr. Hájek, a teacher. He was among those that the teachers remembered helped set up the Civic Forum. It is worth mentioning that the former principal and vice-principal remained at the school and still teach there. Mrs. Veberová said that for two years after the revolution things were not at all easy at the school in terms of relations, and then after another two or three years the situation returned to normal. The former principal, Mr. Brož, saw the 1989 events in similar terms.

Some key players now recall the events with mixed emotions. The question lingers of whether everyone acted properly in the given moment.

it really was so emotional, which sometimes had no true basis. There was so much emotion because now was the time to make changes. They may have even filed some lawsuits. I would say off the top of my head that they did, though at the moment I can't think of any specific ones. But when I think back on it, you mainly experienced it. Maybe you were even very predisposed to condemn something, like, I would never do that. I don't know if I would do it, if I were in that situation. In retrospect, it is hard to imagine that you would do some things the same way even if you were somehow maneuvered into that position.

(Mrs. Kelerová, Chestnut School; qualified to teach pedagogy; currently the deputy mayor of Remízek, 56 years old).

It's apparent that at a certain time at Chestnut it didn't matter who a teacher or person was. All respondents agreed that they did not personally have anything against Mr. Brož or Mrs. Veberová; they were simply on the wrong side at the wrong time. They opted for delaying tactics which the others all saw as a defense of the collapsing regime. In 1989, there were no assessments based on professionalism or approach; their political affiliation played the role.

When the teachers now think back on these events, the implicit question that comes up in the interviews is whether in 1989 a communist could be seen as a good person of a solid nature and a Civic Forum member and demonstrator could be viewed as a "rat". The interpretation of these events is essential. The teachers differ from one another in the degree to which they feel that one was classified according to political affiliation and how great a role political affiliation played in judging a person as a person, and how suddenly the mere fact of political affiliation changed relations in a group, which previously had, according to everyone, worked relatively seamlessly as a whole.

For a tangible idea of the themes linked to the influence of an individual's political orientation on relationships, I have added a table with the statements of teachers who responded to the questions and were active at Chestnut School during that period.

Tab. STATEMENTS ON RELATIONS VIS-À-VIS POLITICAL AFFILIATION DURING 1989 AT CHESTNUT SCHOOL.

Statements of school management representatives before 1989	Statements of Civic Forum representatives (as referred to by their colleagues)	Statements of others
Zavadilová (an excerpt from the 16 February 2011 entry in the author's field journal): *I often think about how some people excuse their shortcomings by claiming to have suffered under totalitarianism.*	Poláková: I basically liked my colleagues and to a certain extent had them figured out. I knew how they taught, their relations to the kids, and this essentially didn't change after the revolution. The ones with some kind of moral compass continued on it that way even after the revolution. It wasn't as if someone decided that he or she would suddenly adhere to a moral code. It was simply a matter of those who behaved morally continued to do so, and those who hadn't ended up changing their colors and going somewhere else and continued to be the same person.	Hloušková: relations became more refined. I'd say that most relations remain solid even today. I'd also note that for some people, who had to step down or no longer continued in the capacity of school management, it took some time for the barriers to fall. I think some people bore it quite well. For instance, those who had been in the communist party did. And nobody would ever bring it up to them. But then, it depends on the person's character: if the person wasn't the kind out to get someone before the revolution, then they wouldn't start doing it after.
Brož: The friends that I have at the school are the same people who were teaching there when I was the principal. So if they quote unquote respected me then, they respect me now. Not because I was the principal or vice--principal, but because I'm a teacher, a person and I am who I am. I get along well with those people. We'll	Poláková: So the Revolution arrived, the Civic Forum was set up and then the school was divided. Some joined the Forum, some didn't. I think it was led by Petr Hájek, who was a contentious, as well as a rebellious figure. [She laughs]. Essentially the former management of the school and others didn't join and they made the wrong choice as history took a different turn. So,	Brožová: (the wife of principal Brož): Believe me when I tell you there were those that I refused to greet and socialize with both then and after. They had really disappointed me. It was so disappointing. November 17 arrived. One of my colleagues had come to me on November 7th or 8th to talk to me about the parade to commemorate the Soviet Revolution, to say that there hadn't

Statements of school management representatives before 1989	Statements of Civic Forum representatives (as referred to by their colleagues)	Statements of others
meet up, go for a coffee or the likes. And for those not interested in being in my company, well, I've no interest in being with them either. There's no pressure from me either way. At my age, I'm certainly not going to force someone to like me.	I remember that Jarmilka Veberová assumed the position of vice-principal for a while, but then had to leave since it all went in a different direction.	been a sufficient number of students from my class in the parade. Then the revolution came and if you had seen and heard that colleague. I just sat there and stared at her with my mouth agape. I simply couldn't understand it.
Brož: I was the vice--principal and then the principal. Then in 1991, actually in 1989 and 1990 people started saying in the teachers' room that I was once in the communist party, or that I still was and how then could I be the principal. And just as it occurred everywhere else, people started flinging mud and started to look for any kind of...	Zabloudilová: They hadn't wanted to allow it in the slightest, and we couldn't even talk about it in the teachers' room. They didn't want to allow for the truth about the revolution and then they utterly changed and became completely different people. For me, that was the worst thing about the revolution. I figured that communists would remain communists and would continue to defend their ideology in the sense that everything is everyone's. But when you look at it that way, the communists remade themselves into the biggest capitalists and already had a head start. Usually those with some skill and drive weren't among those joining the communists, though everyone in our generation was invited to join the communist party, and we all made our lives harder by refusing.	Brožová: As for the relations among teachers, for the most part they were awkward and even sad. What was really unfortunate was that people were loyal to the establishment of the day to the point that sometimes I felt it drove them nuts, and then came the revolution, and you felt that if the Chinese suddenly arrived then people would undergo operations to have slanted eyes. As if they turned right around. Sure, some gradually changed their views, but what really bothered me was those who went from one extreme to the other.

Statements of school management representatives before 1989	Statements of Civic Forum representatives (as referred to by their colleagues)	Statements of others
	Hájek: I'd say that the communists were worried because they didn't know what was going to happen, whether there would be a vendetta of sorts against them, from the party or district or whoever. That was the general sense. It wasn't as if someone was spitting on someone else, certainly not. It was all in the sense that you won, we lost, but there weren't any arguments over it.	Brožová: I was used to, and I think most of us were, that we'd enter the teachers' room and wouldn't care who was there, we'd just say whatever was on our mind. Something like, what a jerk President Husák is. We didn't care who was sitting there. But after the revolution people started being careful of what they said in front of certain people.
	Kelerová: It really isn't possible to have only those lowest-ranked communists...But we felt that the change was going to be so dramatic that there would be a sudden halt to the nonsense that they kept churning out above. When I watch the news today, I ask myself how in the world we could have listened to that. It's about nothing. So everything came tumbling down including the school management. It had to be people who didn't have that in them! I think he [Brož] kind of got hurt. I guess he had no other choice but to insist that "I'm not going to talk to you." He was simply like that, maybe even instructed to say that. I don't know.	Rezková: Then it started amongst us in the teachers' room, since, let me see, well someone simply felt that it was the right occasion. And someone else began to reproach those who were communist party members, even though I was not a party member, so I don't think anyone had anything against me. Then again, I never distinguished between who was in the communist party and who wasn't. I either didn't like people for the way they were or I was fine with how they were and I couldn't care less if they were in the party or not. So I didn't think it was right to distinguish between those who were in the party and those who weren't.

The table clearly shows that the revolutions did in fact profoundly impact the relations at the school. It is apparent from the individual statements that the respondents were seeking some kind of gauge and principles that could provide a satisfactory response to the question: Who is the hero and who is the traitor? Can a former communist be glad that the regime fell and that he can begin his enterprise? Can someone, who obviously conformed the whole time, then establish the Civic Forum? Who has the moral right to say what and how things would be done from then on?

In retrospect, the former principal and vice-principal now think that they were mainly assessed on the basis of their political affiliation and not according to their work or human qualities. Indeed, the revolutionary events automatically brought into question their human quality due to their political affiliation. Yet, according to the teachers, this was the same principle that the communists had applied before 1989.

In terms of relations, those involved spoke of specific instances that help paint a picture of what it was like at that time. The vote of confidence that was held in the hall and, according to all, was an unpleasant confrontation, unquestionably represented an important symbolic moment that depicts the nature of the revolution at Chestnut School. Even the seating order – members of the communist party sat at the chairman's table, the others were in the back – provides ample testimony to what was happening with regards to relations, or better yet, what kind of relations prevailed at the school prior to 1989.

Another apparently confrontational instance was the relationship between the teachers Mrs. Zabloudilová and Mrs. Brožová. According to the testimony, two weeks before the revolution Mrs. Zabloudilová had, in the role of pedagogical advisor, admonished Mrs. Brožová for not ensuring a sufficient number of children at the parade with Chinese lanterns. During the revolution, she had begun to suddenly act in a pro-revolution way and criticized Mrs. Brožová, again for political reasons that she had previously (in Mrs. Brožová's eyes) herself defended.

The whole incident was then obviously very personal: Mrs. Brožová, the wife of the principal, Mr. Brož, the mother of a disabled daughter and not a member of the communist party, follows the revolution which mainly affects her husband, and tries not to lose face. She wears the colors of the Czech flag (her colleagues from Linden School recall this) and yet her husband is written off due to political reasons. It is clear that her statements that the school should have been and should continue to be apolitical are related to this difficult dual role.

In the example of Mrs. Zabloudilová and other colleagues for whom the revolution provided the chance to elicit changes in the school, we again see incidents of those who were up until that point the conforming part of the population. People, who quietly respected the situation at hand during communism, suddenly began to actively come out against the regime. But then they pointed fingers at those who were up until that point fellow travelers on a single boat. The revolution divided the people with a sharp knife.

After these tempests in relations, the situation settled down. Mr. Hájek won the competition for the post of principal. During the interviews he said that "someone" had requested that he enter the competition. This aspect is interesting – none of the three principals of the school who provided an interview admitted wanting to be principal. They had all seen themselves as having heard somebody's call and succumbed to a certain social pressure.

What's more, a number of teachers had repeated another interesting observation that the revolution had occurred all over the district of Lán similarly to how it had happened at Chestnut School. At seven of the eight schools, men had taken over the position of principal and all were gym teachers. Mrs. Veberová added with a laugh that the revolution had taken place in pubs and only men had access to it there because the women were taking care of the kids.

Still another aspect is apparent from the testimonies of some of the teachers affected by 1989. All agreed that the principal's political affiliation had nothing to do with whether the communist leadership welcomed the changes or not. Mrs. Krečmerová, a teacher, recalls that at Beechwood School the revolution took place with great euphoria. Everyone, including the former communist principal, welcomed the changes in unison. This could explain what the teachers were talking about regarding the transferring of teachers to various schools, that those less politically reliable were sent to smaller towns and villages (this appeared in the testimony of Mrs. Rezková who was nearly transferred to Brook School. This would have of course meant that the smaller the school and town, the lower the "political reliability" toward the communist regime. This hypothesis would need to be verified by further research.

Yet according to the respondents, the leadership at Chestnut was mistaken in their view of which way things were going, and in the decisive weeks opted for cautious loyalty to the regime. This came back to haunt them after the revolution had played out.

Everyone agreed that problems did not arise in the classroom. Teachers first began to cautiously abandon words such as "socialistic" and the likes, and gradually modified the curriculum and freed it from ideological information. Some mentioned minor misunderstandings with parents who began insisting that the school not influence their children ideologically. The bad aftertaste from the politicized relationships was gradually replaced by the airy optimism of the acquired freedom, which manifested itself in possibilities to travel, learning foreign languages and broadening horizons as one wanted and an end to wasting times at meetings and political training. Chestnut moved into this free developmental phase that certainly was not without its problems.

Mrs. Zemánková – the Linden School principal

Mrs. Zemánková, the Linden School principal, was born around 1941. Her father was a farmer. "After the war it wasn't good to be a private farmer, so my father lowered his head and joined the communist party, and remained there until his death." Mrs. Zemánková followed in her father's footsteps and joined the communist party, since "that was the prerequisite, so that I could work where I thought I could best serve." She had wanted to be a teacher since childhood and was the first in her entire family to graduate from university. At the pedagogical institute in Brandýs nad Labem she became certified to teach physics, chemistry and workshops. She was hired at Linden School in 1965 and left in 1992 when the new principal Mr. Zámečník became principal, having won the competition in 1991.

According to her and her colleagues, she was a superior chemistry teacher, she liked the work and was glad to take over the position of principal. She ruled with a firm hand, but was also able to put herself in the shoes of her subordinates, and that included political matters.

For instance, in the latter half of the 1980s, the so-called Znojmo Call was announced, according to which all schools in Czechoslovakia were to bind themselves by signature to supply a sufficient number of applicants for military schools. Mrs. Zemánková discussed this action with others at Linden. Two of their colleagues said that she respected that the teachers were against the call and the very principle. The Linden School was one of few schools in Czechoslovakia at that time which refused to sign the call. Mrs. Zemánková apparently said that there would be no repercussions for the decision except that she herself would get in trouble and not get a bonus.

Everyone agrees that she repeatedly stood up for her subordinates when they had some problems of a political nature with parents or with inspectors. For instance, Mrs. Slavíčková said that a parent once came to complain that she wasn't keeping to the syllabus in history, which everyone said was quite often the case. Mrs. Slavíčková, as she herself admitted, would "tell" the students history, and these were generally things that weren't fully in line with the official interpretation of history. Mrs. Zemánková stood up for her and calmed the miffed parent down by explaining that the child probably misunderstood.

After 1989, Mrs. Zemánková remained the principal at Linden until competitions were announced. Unlike the situation at Chestnut, the teachers stood behind her and did not request that she step down. She therefore decided to enter the competition, but said that it was evident in advance that she wouldn't be re-elected due to her communist past, and she was right. After the new principal took over, she left to teach at Chestnut and then retired.

Events of 1989 at Linden School

As is apparent from the recollections of one of the main protagonists of the events at Linden School, the principal Mrs. Zemánková, 1989 in itself did not bring any great changes to the school. In contrast to the situation at the nearby school, the discussion of political events in Linden's staffroom was not taboo. The teachers spoke openly with each other about anything. Those who were in the communist party used words such as "changes had to come, it was unavoidable" to describe the revolutionary events. Mrs. Zemánková commented on the events at that time:

> Well, you know, that wasn't coming from a teacher, but from the principal of the school. I never prevented anyone from going anywhere. If they wanted to take part in a demonstration or assembly, I never prevented them from doing that. But you know, it was a strange kind of feeling because suddenly I saw those people in a slightly different light. Besides being good teachers, they're also good fighters. Now was the time to fight, now was the time to fight. I can still see that teacher making the hand gestures. They were enthusiastic for it.
> (Zemánková, former principal at the Linden School; qualified to teach physics, chemistry and shop; ca. 69 years)

Those who weren't in the party anticipated a more open society. Yet this early thrill in no way impacted relations or what happened at the school. Although the teachers differed in the assessment of the first demonstrations on National Avenue on November 17, 1989, these differences in views did not develop into personal conflicts. The school continued to run.

It's worth mentioning that when describing the events of November 1989, the teachers from Linden consistently used the first person plural – "we didn't overdo it like at Chestnut" etc. They got along as a collective before the revolution and during it. They managed it together; politics didn't divide them into "good and bad" ones. The general strike can serve as an example of how the school was run during the revolution.

Events were normally discussed at the school, even amongst the teachers. When a general strike was announced, the students poured out of the school right at 8 a.m. the teachers had to stop them and tell them the strike wouldn't start until noon. The teachers themselves had a meeting on that day, so they went to strike, and then at 1:00 p.m. came to the meeting.

(Mrs. Grosmanová, Linden School; qualified to teach Czech language and history; currently retired, ca. 56 years old)

During the revolutionary days the teachers said that they combined an open discussion on the events unfolding with their lessons. One respondent even recalls the moment when one girl asked that they just get on with the lesson. The teachers felt that the children were experiencing a certain tension and that it was sometimes too much for them. The children also began to call the teacher "Mrs. Teacher" instead of "comrade".

Currently teaching at Linden are a number of teachers who were at other schools in the district during the days of the revolution. Their thoughts on these events help us to understand what was taking place at the schools. The teachers agreed that the basic structure was the same everywhere. During the weeks and months that followed the revolution, the teachers held a vote of confidence for the principals. The schools where the principals did not receive this confidence then hired new principals; if they did receive it, then competitions were announced for the position in 1991 which anyone could enter. The schools differed in how the teachers reacted to this situation.

If the principal was a big bureaucrat and did what he shouldn't have done, then the teachers let him know what they really felt of him in 1989 during the vote of confidence. On the other hand, there were principals at other schools that worked like people and not like bureaucrats, even though they were unfortunately tagged as bureaucrats and a lot of people made them pay too. And I think they did so unjustly. Some deserved it, others didn't.

(Mr. Řehák, the current principal of Linden school; qualified to teach geography and Russian; ca. 50 years of age)

Following the competitions the situation at the individual schools then went down different paths. For instance, one teacher recalled an event that she felt should not have occurred in a school. "A young principal was hired at our school and he let the students throw the bulletin boards out the window. He said that they served no other purpose and wanted the students to at least do something substantial."

But at Linden School nobody "overdid it". Some teachers contrasted the events at Chestnut – where they felt they overdid it – with those at Linden. Teachers said that a key for understanding the situation at Linden is that nobody cared if someone was in the communist party or not. In assessing people, other criteria played a role: mainly professionalism and human decency that the teachers see as values not linked to politics. In the first months, the Linden School took in those who had been fired elsewhere due to their communist past.

Then those who were in the district were forced to leave. Where could they go? They were linked to Mrs. Zemánková, so they asked that she let them teach at her school. Mr. Buda, he was an inspector, and then there was... he was a clergy secretary: But I can't remember his name. She then convened a meeting, and asked – she didn't decide herself – if we wouldn't mind if they taught here. I really didn't agree with that, but then again I wasn't like, yuk, communist... Mr. Buda then proved to be an excellent teacher, even though he was a pedant.

(Mrs. Grosmanová, Linden School; qualified to teach Czech language and history, currently retired; ca. 56 years old)

As part of the vote of confidence during the early post-revolution period, the teachers at Linden School stood up for Mrs. Zemánková, who remained as principal until the competitions were announced, which she herself entered. Teachers had varied views on this. Some felt that it was insensible since it was clear that she couldn't be re-elected due to her membership in the communist party. Others considered it a bold decision.

It's evident from talking with Mrs. Zemánková that she entered the competition because she was proud of her work and was convinced that she had done a good job leading the school and that it ran smoothly under her leadership. But she also suspected that she didn't have a chance to be selected. And she didn't.

All teachers agreed that the results of the competition were basically known in advance, and that it was a given that the communist leadership had to step down. Mr. Zámečník, at that time a thirty-three-year-old gym teacher from a district school, won the competition. The real drama of 1989 took place at the school after he took over the job.

While respondents from Linden remember the arrival of the new principal quite clearly as a catastrophe, the local chronicle paints a completely different picture:

> On July 1st a new principal won the competition for the post. Mr. Roman Zámečník, born in 1958 in Liberec, and a 1982 graduate of the Pedagogical Faculty at Charles University in Prague will take over leadership of the school. This is the right man for the job, a very progressive individual who has a completely different plan for the development of our school.
> (Chronicle of the town of Remízek, 1991)

It's interesting that at this time the chronicle devotes several pages to the additions planned to be built at Linden School and to praise the new principal, while there is only a paragraph with a very ambiguous conclusion on Chestnut School.

> Just like our old "Mother School", its much younger sister, opened on September 1, 1964, is also currently a witness to many changes. Starting in July of this year there is a change in the principal of this school. Mr. Petr Hájek, born in 1958 and from the nearby town of Poldr has won the competition for this post. He has previously worked as a teacher for this school. Let us presume that this change will be for the best.
> (Chronicle of the town of Remízek, 1991)

The town writes of Linden becoming a flagship of change in the first post-revolutionary period.

Mr. Zámečník completed basic school in the town of Pine, where his family was from. His father tried to make up for the political misdemeanor of having an aunt married off to Germany by joining the communist party. Mr. Zámečník was allowed to study, but owing to his family's profile he only got into a smaller grammar school that he had to commute to, though the school was blessed with a friendly atmosphere unusual for the times. The school was managed in an extremely open way which Mr. Zámečník claimed very much influenced his idea of what an ideal school should be like.

All respondents agreed that there was a very serious conflict after Mr. Zámečník took over as principal, though they disagree about what it mainly concerned. The respondents used a few symbolic instances in their descriptions.

> In the vestibule of the school were concentration camp photographs. It was supposed to be a reverent place, but when a first grader passed through, it didn't leave an overly joyous impression on him. Obviously, there are things that deserve certain homage, but that quote unquote political machinery really got to these kids in this way. And that one-sided view of history, the one-sided requirement of how to interpret it, of how to explain it, how to deal with it, that was very much distilled and obviously also impacted the children.
>
> (Mr. Zámečník, former principal of Linden School; qualified to teach Physical Education; currently the mayor of Grove, ca. 53 years of age).

Mr. Zámečník wanted to create more space for trust and partnership. He quickly replaced the concentration camp pictures with those by the children, and he also declared that children were allowed to go outside during their breaks. Linden School occupies a building of several floors built at the end of the 19th century with relatively narrow corridors and a central stairway. A sidewalk runs along one side of the building, and on the other side there is an open space that can be used as a playground. According to the other teachers, the children previously had not been allowed to go outside because, under such conditions, it could not be ensured that the children could safely get out and back in within a short period of time – not to mention the practical problems of putting on their shoes and taking them back off. The new principal allowed the children to go outside, but then once again prohibited it when – according to the other teachers – he realized it wasn't working. Allegedly there were quite a few of these minor disagreements. Some teachers mentioned that he would arrive late to class and that his conduct as a teacher was less than professional.

Yet these matters did not present as much an obstacle as the contradiction in values and culture. In the beginning, the teachers looked forward to having a new principal. They wanted to see Mrs. Zemánková off in a dignified way and were open to changes. In describing what followed, the teachers used political terminology that teachers at Chestnut had exclusively used for the period preceding 1989. "He wanted to annihilate the old guard", "he took over like a revolutionary", "I had the feeling that it was a communist ploy to bring this place down", "he started to make trouble", etc.

> Yes, Mrs. Zemánková was a communist, but we wanted to part ways with her in a nice way. I expected that education would finally be without all that bureaucracy. Like a new wind. But that first moment when he started in with his Stakhanovite threats that we have to burn for our work...We made fun of that for a long time after. Everyone had those kind of expectations, not just teachers. We thought that there would be an end to protectionism, to corruption... I think the entire society thought that.
>
> (Mrs. Grosmanová, Linden School; qualified to teach Czech language, history, currently retired; ca. 56 years old)

The former principal, Mr. Zámečník, obviously recalled differently what was important for them. His motto was "to introduce a human approach." He wanted the teachers to call the students by their first names, for them to smile at the students, to greet them and to respond to their greetings. He tried to open the school to the public and present it outwards.

In response to the question on the nature of the conflict, teachers spoke of professional matters – in their view it was a different idea of what the school should be like and how things should be done in the school. They felt that Mr. Zámečník brought with him a certain chaos – to the order and discipline of the school that worked like a clock. Suddenly a new wind blew in that, in the teachers' view, destroyed that which should have been preserved. Moreover, he introduced things that went against the teachers' professional convictions.

> For instance, I was in the workshop, which was in the cellar, and next to us was the playground. I taught half the class and the other class had gym. Those kids were out of control for twenty minutes, scoffing at the kids in the workshop for having to saw while they could run around. Then the principal, who taught the gym class, came twenty minutes late, kicked a ball to them, and it was settled. Or they would head for the stadium and before they got there the class would end so they'd have to turn around and come back. I'd never seen this type of approach in all my years teaching. How can someone tell me

that I have to do something and then act in that kind of way. Well, there were personal issues between us because I didn't like his approach.

(Zemánková, former principal at Linden School; qualified to teach physics, chemistry and shop; ca. 69 years of age)

The culmination of the slowly developing conflict was an episode concerning the distribution of bonuses. Under Mrs. Zemánková it had always been done transparently and for extra work. Mr. Zámečník hired a new English teacher and she received all the money earmarked for bonuses herself, even before she had started to teach. What's more, she was always absent. In those days the German teacher would take over the English teacher's half of the class when she wasn't there. At the mid-year the German teacher brought a bottle to the staffroom saying that she is celebrating her 50th time covering for the English teacher.

The tension culminated with a mass exodus of some teachers from the school. Five or six teachers left Chestnut when Mr. Neuman was asked to be vice-principal. Everyone agreed that the principal Mr. Hájek and Mr. Neuman did not have the same political views, but they agreed on Chestnut's concept of sports education that the school was heading towards.

Mr. Neuman accepted the offer and a number of teachers came with him, including former principal Mrs. Zemánková. This is quite surprising since membership in the communist party was at Chestnut School a primary reason for the revolution. But the teachers knew that Mrs. Zemánková was a superb teacher, and that overweighed any misgivings at the crucial moment.

The transfer to Chestnut also seemed the most natural since the histories of the two schools were linked from the very beginning.

Yet when Mrs. Zemánková thinks back on the transfer, the picture seemed a lot more dramatic. She said that she still regrets leaving and that all she did at Chestnut School was close herself in her office and teach. It is clear from the interviews that these events are still a difficult topic of conversation for her.

I still regret having to leave [she cries and is then silent]. I was the first there and was the last to leave. Even now when I think back to it I get upset. Even after all those years. I lived for that school, both figuratively and literally. I still have a hard time coming to terms with it.

(Zemánková, former principal at the Linden School, qualified to teach physics, chemistry, shop, ca. 69 years)

Other teachers transferred to the schools from surrounding villages. According to the respondents, twenty of the fifty-three teachers left over the course of two years.

> Even during communism the school was able to provide the children with moral values. We certainly didn't teach them how to steal or lie... I can want to rectify, to suppress old things, but I need to know how to rectify them, not just sweep them away... they tried to sweep away the old structures... A lot of people from a good collective, both party members and non-members, left – many went to the school nearby. I did not hold the same political views as Mr. Zámečník, even though I was for the revolution.
>
> (Mrs. Hartová, Linden School; qualified to teach first-level students and special education; 57 years old).

In retrospect, former principal Mr. Zámečník's assessment of the situation did not differ that much from his colleagues. He was left with a disappointing feeling that it didn't work out:

> There's some truth in that I was a young guy, a little green, and the teachers were experienced... On the other hand, I tried to act properly towards them; I let them continue to teach at the school... I simply took it as a certain change, and that they could obviously continue to work there in peace. I tried to pull them into the event.
>
> (Mr. Zámečník, former principal of Linden School; qualified to teach Physical Education; currently the mayor of Grove, ca. 53 years of age).

Mr. Zámečník today admits that the post-revolutionary period brought with it a certain change in terms of respect and borders.

The teachers who left Linden met with different fates. Some of them returned to Linden after Mr. Zámečník left to become mayor, others remained at their new places of work. Today, the teachers are even conciliatory in revisiting the situation.

> In retrospect it is evident that he was right in some things, and that we were right in some things... Obviously within three months the kids weren't allowed to go outside, since it wasn't working out; they would have brawled with each other. But on the other hand... It was his idea to make classrooms in the attic. Mrs. Zemánková said that it would collapse... And today there are beautiful classrooms. So a lot of things worked out and many didn't work out.
>
> (Mrs. Grosmanová, Linden School; qualified to teach Czech language and history; currently retired ca. 56 years old)

Thus the revolution also impacted Linden, but with a greater delay and with a different dynamic. At Linden the conflict was more of a cultural nature, a change in the basic paradigm in society appeared in a conflict of values that culminated in the voluntary departure of almost half of the faculty.

Most of the respondents distinguished between the hectic post-revolutionary period and the 'normal' life that started after things calmed down. The conflict caused by Mr. Zámečník's actions as principals was in their view still the fruit of the revolution. After a few years the situation settled down and 'normal' life started. In assessing the events of that period, Mrs. Zemánková, the former principal, was assisted by a conceit from her field – chemistry:

> When you blend that mixture it continues to develop. It takes a long time to break down into individual components, into individual levels, just like in chemistry. Well, unfortunately, I feel like in 1990 it kind of came to the surface, though I don't want to say from the bottom. But such a level of people, who had fewer scruples. Less tact in communication. They were more aggressive. It just didn't seem right to me.
>
> (Zemánková, former principal at the Linden School; qualified to teach physics, chemistry and shop; ca. 69 years of age)

What caused the problems? Greater openness or fewer scruples? The fundamental question at Chestnut School is "who is the hero and who is the traitor?" At Linden the question is more about respect and decency. What is a contemporary person of character like?

The situation at both schools has changed a lot since then. After 1989, Chestnut School underwent a great boom. So many children enrolled in the first class that the school had to use other facilities for classes, e.g. a classroom at a local vocational school. Yet presently there is greater interest in Linden School, and Chestnut seems to be looking for a new path.

Of the teachers who left Linden School during the Zámečník era, one respondent returned ten years later, i.e. during the boom. The relations between teachers at both schools have gradually stabilized.

What changed after 1989

A whole wave of changes came after 1989, and it was evident from the interviews that the social changes influenced and continue to considerably influence what happens in schools today. The teachers at both schools markedly agreed in their assessment of the social changes.

Society changed

The teachers agreed that the acquired **freedom** that came with the fall of communism was a great relief for them. The teachers used expressions such as "the tension fell from us", "we could speak freely without repression" or "we were free to say what we think".

The first years after the revolution was the dominant theme and everyone very much made use of the freedom. But the teachers also spoke about the unbridled freedom of the first years after the revolution led to the decrepitude that society finds itself in today. According to the teachers, society missed the chance to properly handle freedom, and that too much freedom, the borderless kind, is instead detrimental. Sometimes even more severe statements were made: "We were all stuffed full of democracy, but we didn't know what it amounted to." Teachers asked: "Where is the border? Who will tell you what is still ok and what isn't?" The teachers found in society "great sovereignty, but no respect".

In their view, too much freedom led to a certain vulgarization of the entire society. This appeared in numerous instances – from a feeling of danger on the streets to the rise in drug use. Two respondents said that in 1989 those who ended up winning were the ones with "long elbows who knew how to stir things up and make a lot of noise. They promised a lot and did nothing." Another added with a certain dose of satisfaction that one of the teachers at Chestnut School, who in 1989 was one of the loudest proponents of change, opted for early retirement, "disgusted" with the way things were.

In the subtext of remarks of former communist party members who worked at Linden School you could sense a kind of grappling with the implicit question: "Is this what you really wanted?" Even those who were not in the party seemed to be saying: "We had such high hopes and it ended up falling so short." I sensed during the interviews that they were amazed that such a shortcoming was even possible.

According to the teachers, the main problem consisted of the value system radically changing – with society ruled by **money and success** that became the main objective and meaning of life. Obviously, this influences the relationships between children and parents as well as everyday events in schools. The teachers felt that it would still be acceptable if it were just a case of needing to accumulate things. But the biggest problem was that the end justifies the means – what is important is to have money, not to earn it in an honorable way. The teachers expressed the view that society considers sharp elbows, and not dignified work, essential. "Whoever doesn't steal is stealing from his family," was the motto that endured from the communist years, or "in the past when someone was said to be of solid character it meant something." Today none of that is true. If someone is nice, kind, a solid character, then he's an idiot. People took their rights, but not the responsibilities.

> So they [the children] see that actually the entire society is influenced by money whether we admit it or not. I think that the children see, or they may even talk about it at home, that he who is well off is the one with the sharp elbows, who's arrogant, who outwits the others... And I think that this is an unhealthy atmosphere in society. That communist period was so incredibly restricted. It didn't let people naturally compete. The rules were clearly set and this wasn't right either. There was a specific planned order, those people were confined by something, they simply couldn't do anything. And then after 1989 it seems to me that those people completely thoughtlessly or without any moral compass or whatever pushed their way forward and whoever had the chance, they essentially – I don't want to say stole... society just took an unhealthy path. And I think that's the root problem. That's why people behave the way they do.
>
> (Krečmerová, Chestnut School; studied to be a Czech-language and art teacher; today teaches English, 51 years old).

Who is the modern-day hero? What should we be like and how should we try to raise children? That's the question that resonated from the interviews. Teachers are a tad in the role of Don Quixote in that they continue to believe in traditional values and decency, while the surrounding world is changing and beginning to profess other values. Yet teachers are the ones that this transformation very much concerns. The students get into situations on a daily basis in which they experience first hand the conflict in values and the change in paradigm. In a world in which the main gauge of anything essential is money, it's hard to convince children that even things like relationships, education and thoughtfulness are valuable and meaningful.

> When I said, well then, if you want to be a mason, then you can be a clever mason. Or do you think you have to be dumb? And he said, that's right,

but how much do you make and how much am I going to make. And I said, I know I don't have much, but at least I know something, and nobody can take that away from me. So education dropped down a peg. It's not needed since everyone hustled something somewhere, sold something, made money or didn't have to do a thing, so something like education wasn't needed. It dropped down a peg.

(Mrs. Slavíčková, Linden School; qualified to teach history; ca. 70 years of age)

The main problem of a society based on performance and money is that the profit then isn't covered by adequate effort. Instead, the goal is to make a profit without much effort. Quick and easy. So the result doesn't have to correspond to the effort exerted.

According to the teachers, the transparency aspect also plays a role in this type of society. And what the children see outside the school, they bring into its building:

Something is always brewing under the counter and then all of a sudden it's made public. So I think that, all told, this was happening at the school. That those children know that without self-confidence, which often isn't even that healthy, they didn't have a chance to make it. That they see it in adults and all around. This has a great impact on them.

(Mrs. Okázalová, Linden School; qualified to teach history, ca. 42 years of age)

Such a society then creates "the borders for the game" – the children and parents, just like the teachers, merely move within these borders. In their view, teachers seek a way to shift these borders a little. Their frustration is then related to the fact that it is difficult to move the borders and that they don't feel authorized to do it and don't know if anybody even wants them to do it. They lack the authorization from a higher power or the mere feeling of consent with general expectations from the school.

In the interviews the teachers also sought the reasons which this situation has arisen. They named a whole range of reasons – from a lack of faith in capitalism as a whole to its application in the Czech Republic. Although the teachers clearly considered it a relief to be done with communism, all generations of teachers seemed to agree that the newly established order was not good. One teacher recalled the revolutionary slogan from the winter of 1989: "The aim of the revolution was socialism with a human face, not capitalism." Doubts were thereby cast on the new system itself.

Some teachers even reflected upon the role of the West or, in other words, what we had brought over from the West. For instance, former principal Mrs. Zavadilová recalled how one of her colleagues had travelled to London before 1989 and returned shocked at how rude the children in the schools had been there. Now she feels that the situation is the same here.

Other teachers don't blame the West, but perceive what a real opening of society brought, how the fine web of the means of communication has changed and how their world has changed.

> Suddenly we could sing and do and say whatever we wanted, and there disappeared that secrecy and quaintness and you could say anything and everything suddenly became more crude and lost the more subtle senses, that fragility, and those children were rolling in so much information. I'm not talking about the years right after the revolution, those were wonderful, but after that.
>
> (Mrs. Poláková, Chestnut School; qualified to teach Russian and music; today teaches English, ca. 45 years old).

The school and society moved from one **extreme to the other**. The teachers themselves created during the interviews polar categories such as strictness x looseness, order x school of games, democracy x chaos, totalitarianism x democracy. It is as if a certain type of extremism in the school and society remained, but that the polarity of the assessing marks, under which it works, were reversed. I will give two examples of many:

> After twenty years I find out that those kids don't know how to work. All those obligatory stints of manual labor were good for the students. But they suddenly did away with it, saying that the school is only here to teach the kids. But it's also good when you teach the kids that potatoes are harvested two weeks a year and that suddenly there are so many that the agriculture workers can't manage it all and that it's a good thing for the students to spend a half day or three days there and see for themselves that the work is really hard and that it's better to study and not end up in agriculture.
>
> (Mrs. Zabloudilová, Chestnut School; qualified to teach mathematics; currently a freelancer, ca. 61 years of age)

I remember one scene, at that time they were showing the film *Jesus* – an epic film. And Petra Zabloudilová as a Christian… and I don't know what the other teachers were doing for it. But I was, for instance, going over the music, and then I went to see Mr. Hrabě and he sent me to see Mr. Zajíc, who was on the board of Nova Television, and also a Christian. And since I know nothing about it, I went to see him and had him explain everything. I even went to see him because of Christmas carols, since they were only words to me that we repeated, and I didn't understand them, so I jotted it down in a notebook and passed it around. So, I prepared for that Jesus and I told the kids what had happened, what pictures were there, and I tried – because that was a topic that nobody knew anything about, and if they knew then they weren't allowed to speak about it. I can still see Petra Zabloudilová, how, before the film started, she stood up and in this tragic trembling voice began to tell them "And now we have freedom and now Jesus is with us," and I watched and said to myself – my god, now the ideology will come from the other side.

(Mrs. Poláková, Chestnut School, qualified to teach Russian, music, today teaches English, ca. 45 years old).

In the first case, as a reaction to the previous obligatory student work stints, the participation of children in agriculture was completely suppressed, which is, however, detrimental to the educational objectives that could be fulfilled with their help.

In the second case, the situation is reversed – although the theme of religion is now allowed, it is sometimes as ideological as the themes linked to life in communism used to be. The teachers perceive this reversing of polarity very strongly. It is as if the political changes necessarily meant that everything had to change, even that which worked well.

The former principal, Mr. Zámečník, who now reflects on the entire situation from the position of the town's mayor, poses the following question:

Where is the border between democracy and chaos? [...] Perhaps the path to democracy, to a discussion, turned into something that was precariously close to being out of control. There is the need to define where that boundary is and who is the authority in the society – the parent, entrepreneur, teacher, student… The roles are largely given, but not respected. Thus the society in general, which had not been raised in a democracy for a long time, does not know how to deal with this democracy.

(Mr. Zámečník, former principal of Linden School; qualified to teach Physical Education; currently the mayor of Grove, ca. 53 years of age).

Society also went from one extreme to another in the extent which it observed the rules that it itself had established. Teachers perceive here a change in the sense, objective and values. Yet they also sense that in comparison with the past, the ways that we relate to these values often changed.

> I would say that we are deformed in that there were some rules during communism and, actually, these rules were broken and more or less not respected since this was something dictated and the people didn't agree with it. But that inner feeling that we should still break the rules remains within us. This despite the fact that the rules were passed democratically.
>
> (Mr. Zámečník, former principal of Linden School; qualified to teach Physical Education; currently the mayor of Grove, ca. 53 years of age).

The teachers feel that this has unfortunate consequences. It is worth mentioning that different generations of teachers had a similar view of this, regardless of their prior or present political convictions.

The question at hand is how this came to be. Aiding our understanding of this situation are the specific recollections of teachers, who reflect upon this fundamental shift in a paradigm within which the entire society moves. It seems that some teachers tried to set some boundaries to the newly acquired freedom, but in the early years following the revolution these attempts failed.

> We went to the training and there some teachers drew their attention to the fact that our cinemas were suddenly being bombarded by all this stupidity from America and the West, and that our television was suddenly filled with these Ninja Turtles, who would just kept pulling out their swords and beating up everything. We were keen to have everything we didn't have, and for our kids to have it, and of course our enthusiasm subsided, as did the kids', and those parents didn't know what it really all amounted to, like with those Ninja Turtles... what's the point? So they kind of underestimated it and now we suddenly saw that those children have, for instance... I'll tell you: one parent said, they wake, they're scared, they call out from their sleep, they don't sleep well... Well, then you find out that they let the kid watch that for three quarters of an hour, or even an hour. I don't even know how long, but nobody said anything to him about it, so he has a completely different take on it. So we were at that training session, and we wanted to draw attention to it. And there was a woman there about 50 or 55, maybe she wanted to please someone. So we were living with the impression that since democracy was

here, everyone had a chance to say something about it, since democracy meant that I can say whatever I want, doesn't it? [she laughs]. So we said our piece and she tore into us like you wouldn't believe. That we wanted communism back and that we wanted, I don't know, censorship and that it wasn't right for us to bring that up here. We just stared at her. We couldn't even believe that someone could say that there. So everyone shut their ears and let it be. And now, ten years later, from 2000, you suddenly hear it gradually discussed how the violence on television will impact the next generation.

(Mrs. Friedrichová, Chestnut School; qualified to teach natural history; currently retired, ca. 66 years old)

One point of interest is that if we were to quantify the teachers responses, most talked about what had changed in society. It is clearly a topic that bothers them since it has immediate consequences in terms of what they experience daily in school. Indeed, the children and their parents have also changed.

The lines between the changes in relationships and culture of the entire school are partly changes in society and partly the new reality in which teachers and students have been operating since the reform in 2004. I will first present the teachers views of the reform and then, with a knowledge of the external facts, I will return to an analysis of changes in the school culture – and specifically to relations between teachers, parents and students.

What the reform gave and what it took away

The aim of this research was not primarily to ascertain the effects of the reform of the educational system and of its individual parts on teachers, but to capture the changed situation in schools from the teachers' perspective. Nevertheless, the teachers spoke about the reform during the interviews, especially about its parts that directly influence their everyday teaching practices. The teachers characterize the first several years following the revolution as a search. First, they themselves cautiously changed the syllabus, then new textbooks began to gradually appear. Yet the teachers did not see any changes initiated from above in either the content or methods of teaching until 2004, when the educational reform arrived. The reform from 2004 brought great changes to Czech education, mainly due to the decentralization of the curriculum. Based on centrally provided recommendations – of the basic educational program – the individual schools prepared their own school educational programs, i.e. a complete curriculum for all subjects and grades. Also introduced were so-called cross-sectional educational themes that were to pervade all subjects and enrich the curriculum with its pedagogical dimension. Their application differed on the various types of schools, but the goal was to cultivate the upbringing of a democratic citizen able to think in European and global contexts – a medial, multicultural and environmental education (The General Educational Program for Basic Education, 2010).

The School Educational Programs (SEP) were developed by the teachers themselves at each school. The teachers approached them differently at each school – sometimes commissions for the individual departments were created, at other times specific teachers were tasked with drafting the plan for the given subject, and sometimes the principals played the main roles. According to off-the-record information respondents shared with me, some schools even adopted the school educational programs from other schools.

During the period in which the school education programs were being prepared, the amount of work increased significantly, though there was no extra pay for it, as the schools didn't receive any extra money for it. This was the source of much discontent (Moree, 2008).

The teachers at Chestnut School worked on the programs divided into teams and obviously – like everywhere else – without remuneration for this extra work. According to vice-principal Mrs. Hloušková, work on the programs brought some individuals in the work teams closer together, elsewhere it inflamed already smoldering disputes. Principal Hájek said that "the idea was good, but the execution was horrible." Most teachers, from all generations, agreed with this assessment. In addition, the principal was obviously also bothered by that managerial aspect.

> I had to force the teachers to do something even though there was no remuneration for it. They were actually doing in their own way scholarly work, compiling something, and I didn't have a crown to give them. That was malicious.
>
> (Mr. Hájek, the current principal of Chestnut School; qualified to teach geography and physical education; ca. 56 years of age)

The reforms were prepared for in a slightly different way at Linden. Principal Řehák said that the reform was not necessary since they had already taught in a reformed way prior to 2004. The preceding principal had, in his view, prepared everything well, and when the obligation arrived to create the SEP, they were able to just take the changes that they had already more or less made and incorporate them into another document. Yet this process obviously bothered many teachers, since the school already had the process of creating something new behind it, and this phase was perceived *de facto* like a new administrative burden that would not bring a deeper change, but just take time away from truly important work.

All teachers, regardless of gender and age, feel that the reform failed. As in the matter of social changes, most of the teachers agree on this. The teachers' disapproval of the reform is not in the spirit that they don't think educational system should remain unchanged. On the contrary – everyone felt the need for change, but the way it was done brought more negatives than positives. Intensified by structural changes in education, the reform in their view led to the overall degradation of education. While some causes stem directly from the reform, others are a kind of by-product of demographic and other changes. Teachers offered some explanations of the current status:

The **fragmentation of the curriculum** stems directly from the reform. Anyone can prefer his or her own agenda which they believe are more essential than others. But this shouldn't happen at a basic school. The teachers felt that a primary school should provide a clear foundation, a basic education, and that there is no room for experimentation. The results should be clear.

> At any time, and under any regime, you'll always find those that were en-
> thusiastic for what was happening. If we take, for instance, those plans that
> every school had to draw up, I said from the start that they were absolutely
> nonsense. We're a primary school. All primary schools throughout the coun-
> try and perhaps all over the world have the same syllabus content. The same
> level of knowledge that is achievable, that is optimized. It's like the case of
> a theater performance: you'll always have people in the audience screaming
> how wonderful it is. That was the case at our school. And today they're start-
> ing to realize that it isn't as optimized as they had wanted.
>
> (Mr. Brož, Chestnut School, qualified to teach chemistry and workshops,
> ca. 67 years old)

Uncertainty regarding the expected performance was the main peda- gogical argument made by teachers. The question obviously is how and in which time intervals was the expected performance to be defined. Yet the teachers agreed that if they didn't know the objective, i.e. the expected performance, then they couldn't move toward it. The teachers felt that it would help if the expected performance was defined for every year and not every three years. A three-year interval complicates the transparency of the whole system and makes it difficult to compare schools. This becomes apparent e.g. when students have to move.

Paradoxically, the non-existence of clearly defined expected performances bears with it the fact that the curriculum is overfilled. For instance, one teacher mentioned that although one hour of math was cancelled, other classes were introduced and that the children spent much more time in school. This creates stress for the kids since they then only study and do schoolwork, and don't have time to unwind. Then their behavior is worse.

The teachers were also disappointed that the **changes were more of a cosmetic nature**: It used to be called the pedagogical goal, today it's called competencies, but it's the same thing. The reform formally requires that the teacher do something that he or she does not agree with, and there's not time for what the teachers are calling for – to raise the quality of education.

> Essentially, the teacher is accustomed to teaching. But then we are asked to write research papers on top of that. We don't know how to do that. What's the point for him to write up competencies. It's always about that same person, how he will approach the children, and not that he's going to analyze it. I did this and that. I'm going to treat the children well and put all my energy into, but I certainly won't prepare for it the evening before. I obviously prepare for the material, but not in the sense in which they prescribe me these competences that we should work on. When I was inspected, I was supposed to fill out which competences were worked on during the class. I had to take a paper, template and look at what to fill out. I think that there should be quality teaching aids, that the money earmarked for reforms was wasted on a lot of useless material. It would have been better if it went toward school equipment and learning aids for the kids and even for that training of yours we went to [the respondent took part in a training session I had held for teachers – author's note]. It would have been much better to invest the money that way than into the SEP, since none of the teachers, even though they created the SEP, ever got the money. But it's not about the money for teachers. I don't mean it that way. I just mean that the money was very poorly invested.
>
> (Mrs. Kučerová, Linden School; qualified to teach first-level students and andragogy; ca. 39 years old).

Not only does the situation lead to the paradox of "seeking out those proper competences when the inspector comes," but also to the fact that the teachers can't use in the classes what they created. Several teachers mentioned in this context the creation of so-called digital teaching materials (DTM). These are preparations for certain topics that the teachers make to activate the children and so that other colleagues can have the teaching materials available for their subjects. The teachers had to create these digital materials which resulted in several problems. Everyone created the digital materials in their own way, and so the possibility for other colleagues to use them was greatly reduced. Even if it was gradually enlarged and the digital materials could be used in teaching, their usability depends upon how well the school is equipped, since the teachers were already working in them with an internet browser and other electronic aids. During the research, Chestnut School was participating in one of the European projects, within the framework of which the school was able to provide for a sufficient degree of technical equipment. Up until that point a great skepticism prevailed regarding the DTMs; what's more, their application would not have been possible without the extra efforts of those in charge of improving the school's technical state. This type of experience then obviously results in teachers distrusting the reform. Indeed, they didn't have any reason to believe from their experiences that it would bring about an improvement. Instead, they perceived it as a process that increased the number of senseless obligations, of which at the moment nobody had any.

The reform also meant a loosening of the **methods** used to teach, in other words it opened and increased the chance of teaching in other ways. A greater degree of creativity is one of the few positive aspects that teachers saw in the reform. At the same time, however, the approach to the methods apparently divided the teachers.

The main topic at each of the schools was the methods. Teachers at Chestnut see the reform as a symbol for the end of order in schools. Older teachers perceive it as pressure on them to change their ways and to liven up lessons with projects, presentations and other activities. They consistently do this to build up their teaching portfolio which is evaluated.

These very activities are also important in the portfolio. Even though the teachers try to introduce new methods into their lessons, they doubt that they have much effect or improve the quality of their teaching. Instead, they feel the opposite is true. In their view, activities such as projects increase the social injustice element: not all parents can afford to pay for trips, and as a result their kids can't take part in all social activities. Projects and trips also disturb the normal course of the school year, and trips are to the detriment of actual learning.

Above all, the older teachers link the new methods with a loss of discipline (the students can leave the class whenever they want and that disrupts the teaching). The new methods tend more to lead the kids to play, which they enjoy, but don't learn anything. According to the older teachers, the children should learn to remember certain types of skills, without which neither discussions nor projects are possible.

> Lessons should have some kind of order. If I'm teaching art where they can draw for a half hour or hour by themselves, then it doesn't matter if they sit in a circle. But when I'm teaching one of the main subjects such as Czech or math and such things when one thing is linked to the next, and when a student walks out of the class and is gone for a quarter hour, maybe to the bathroom, or so he says, since they can leave whenever they want without asking, then that is a disruption. It disrupts the teacher's lesson, and the children are affected by it the most since they miss out on something they need to understand what comes after. So I don't like these new systems. I guess I'm just old-school.
>
> (Mrs. Staňková, Chestnut School; qualified to teach math and art, currently retired and teaching at an art school for children; ca. 73 years of age)

> At least that's how it was formulated, that the material shouldn't just be crammed into them, that they should learn in other ways as well. But in my view there are things that you really just have to learn. First there needs to be a skeleton of sorts, and only then can you add muscles to it. But they have to learn those basic things, to tough it out and learn it.
>
> (Mr. Šlosarová, Chestnut School; qualified to teach history, art, ca. 48 years old)

In the eyes of the older teachers, the young teachers are responsible for introducing the new methods at Chestnut School, which is one of the reasons there is tension in relations between the generations. Since among the younger teachers at Chestnut school who started teaching there about five years ago there was only one respondent who agreed to be interviewed, it is difficult to draw more general conclusions from her responses. It seems, however, that even teachers from the younger generation did not want to completely abandon the established order.

In my view, even that knowledge previously associated with cramming the students full of information is needed. Simply put, without it nothing is possible. The children, of course, are more interested in projects and talking about things, and they learn to work more independently. I certainly see progress in that reports used to be shoddy; they would print it out somewhere in the school and read it. Today, at least in my class, they have to do a lot more work on it and must have a certain independent slant and put more into it, and so on. It teaches them to look at it from a far broader perspective and think it over more. Not just print it out and read it. They are certainly learning to speak more, but the traditional knowledge is going down. For instance, at the moment I'm preparing the children for the Biology Olympiad and there are things that they simply don't know because they don't have it ingrained in them by the intensive knowledge-based lessons. I know that we went over it because I taught them it, but they don't have it embedded in them. That's because it's in different contexts.

(Mrs. Bílková, Chestnut School; originally a social worker, today teaches geography, natural history and informatics; ca. 35 years old).

All teachers thus agree that "cramming" is necessary, but the question is how much and in what way should children learn this way.

One of the reasons that this topic bothers teachers is that they all feel that the level of education is dropping. A telling example consists of the oft repeated statements of a number of older teachers from both schools that they can no longer use tests prepared several years ago from the exact sciences, such as math and chemistry, for the same age group of children since they are too difficult for children today.

I see how it's going downhill. What I taught you and what you knew, I can sign my name right under that. It seems to me that the leaving exam is half as difficult. I did the whole thing in an hour. I downloaded it from the internet and felt like the examples were what I'd been giving to 8th and 9th graders. That was twenty or twenty-five years ago, and now they're making out of it who knows what and it costs millions, but I feel like you knew almost more at primary school. It's all going downhill, completely downhill. [She was referring to leaving-exam exams from 2010 – author's note.]

(Mrs. Zabloudilová, Chestnut School; qualified to teach mathematics; currently a freelancer, ca. 61 years of age)

At Linden School the new methods are not an issue. Everyone agreed that the style of the teacher's work did not dramatically change with the reform and that the new methods are more entrenched in the school. Only the organization of projects, which take a lot of time, remains a question.

For the most part they see the possibility to carry out projects as beneficial. Yet a number of them know from experience that it can easily collapse if the entire school is not in favor of the projects and feel that they are an important part of the educational process. For if some of the teachers held back the projects, and others tried to create something with the children, a paradoxical situation could arise that, according to one respondent, actually occurred at his former workplace. As part of the project, the children memorized chemistry formulas on which they were to be graded – they would get for it good grades which their parents were expecting, which appear on the report cards and, therefore, by which their success would be assessed. If the projects are not perceived by all those involved as an equal part of the education, they are for some teachers merely a game that takes up time needed for normally taught material.

Possibilities for the reform's creative use are limited by the high head-count of classes which did not change with the reform. Projects and other creative types of activities are, according to teachers, very difficult with high numbers of children.

One fundamental practical that many teachers complained about came from the fragmentation of the curriculum: problems related to **students moving**. Each school arranges the obligatory subject material into different grades and sometimes even in a different order. In terms of continuity, moving then often has a catastrophic effect on the student's education. It makes it very hard for students to change schools.

> One girl entered our school in the seventh grade. I teach seventh-grade history and I was already at the 17th century, the beginning of the 17th century. So I looked in her notebook and she had left off at, I don't know, the twelfth or thirteenth century. So it means she skipped 300 or 400 years of Czech history.
> (Mrs. Veberová, Chestnut School; qualified to teach Russian and Czech; also teaches German, ca. 58 years old).

Another teacher gave the example of a child who had German up to the seventh grade in her earlier school and then after moving had to start with English at a slightly advanced level.

The reform was also accompanied by considerable **teacher training**. Yet such training was often of a dubious quality that did not satisfy the actual needs of teachers and did not reflect the specific situation of teachers and their students. One respondent used the example of moving students to demonstrate the remoteness of the training's content from the reality in school.

And now imagine that we'd say, yeah, that's nice, that school is preparing in its own way. This one this way, that one that way. And now the kid's parents want to move away and they put the kid in a different school. The kid had chemistry at our school in the seventh grade and won't have chemistry in the new school or vice versa. And they're going to want chemistry from him. In the seventh grade. And you know what they told us? So they simply can't move. That was the answer. What can you say to that?

(Mrs. Friedrichová, Chestnut School; qualified to teach natural history; currently retired, ca. 66 years old)

The contradiction between the teachers' actual situation and that which they learn at training sessions as part of their further education is a very sensitive matter. They approach it differently at each of the monitored schools.

Chestnut leaves it up to the teachers when and for which training they enroll. Linden motivates its teachers and always provides in its annual report an overview of the courses that its teachers have completed. Yet at both schools the experiences are quite similar – among the offered courses are those that always prove to be of high quality and that the teachers like to attend, although there are also plenty of those that don't bring anything new. From the offer that the teachers receive, it is very difficult to choose a course that is guaranteed to be of a high quality. At present the schools are showered with a wide range of offers, of which it is extremely difficult to estimate the course's quality in advance.

Since the teachers are not satisfied with the reform, they obviously ask **who is responsible for it.** Linden's principal spoke of the structural transformation of the education system. In his eyes it wasn't about the complete decentralization of curricula, but that the so-called branch management was done away with, as were the district school offices. He feels it provides the chance to work with other colleagues, even regarding content; today, however, schools only have their authorities and they don't concern themselves with content. Although Linden School has solid relations with its authority (and nobody from Chestnut complains about the relations either), in more remote parts of the region it is often worse, and discussions about content are not held at all.

Teachers agreed that even though administrative tasks were reduced for a while after 1989, they increased dramatically with the school reform, which runs precisely counter to the desired effect of the reform. The reform was supposed to increase the quality of teaching, but so far teachers only spend unpaid time doing administrative work and they actually have less time to prepare lessons than before the reform.

In addition to the extra administrative work, the teachers also have to deal with the fact that each school had to prepare the reform itself, which greatly increased the administrative load. Some dryly stated that "they had to do the hard work that the Pedagogical Research Institute had been doing for years." This brought with it considerable instability and distrust in the entire system.

In short, the teachers have the feeling that they are investing a greater amount of energy into education, which has yielded increasingly worse results – they speak of the **degradation of education**. In their view this occurs due to several reasons that are more linked to the entire education system than to the reform. The eight-year grammar schools grab all the talented students from the basic schools, where the average kids remain. There is then a lack of the "draft horses", the students able to pull the entire group forward. That is one of the reasons why second-level students get worse marks than before.

The consequences of the existence of these eight-year grammar schools would not have been so severe if fewer kids had left for them. Since the second level of schools are currently filled with classes with fewer kids (due to lower birth rates the years the students were born) and the grammar schools also need to survive, they lower the bar for admitting kids, both after the fifth year of primary school and during the entering exams to a four-year grammar school. The result of this is that more average and less talented kids remain at the basic schools. The teachers feel that grammar schools should only be for especially talented kids and not for kids who merely do well. The boundary to leave for an eight-year gymnasium should in their view lie elsewhere.

To top it all off there are private schools where affluent and ambitious parents in particular can send their kids. According to information provided by Chestnut vice-principal Mrs. Hloušková, in 2010 there were 50% more open spots than applicants at secondary schools.

There's such a mess in schooling. I have a friend with a son, he's already older now, but just imagine, he got into an economics school, then a half year later he transferred to another economics school that seemed easier to him. He ended the year with two Fs, in chemistry and something else, and all he could say was what do I need chemistry for since I don't even like it, and she accepted that. At the midterm he got another F, so she enrolled him in a private school where there were only eight kids in the class, each with his own computer. The truth is that she paid twenty thousand crowns, but that boy, he passed his leaving exam. Otherwise he wouldn't have. That aspect of the education system really bothers me.

(Mrs. Veberová, Chestnut School; qualified to teach Russian and Czech, also teaches German, ca. 58 years old).

Teachers who had taught at private schools spoke of similar situations:

They pay for the leaving exam there too. It was a common occurrence for them to pay for the leaving-exam certificate. I don't know if this was also the case of the school where I was teaching, but it was such a schocking experience that nobody could ever get me to work at a school like that again. I tested one final-year student there, not during the leaving exam, but at the midterm since he had too many absences, because the students barely go to school there, so he had to take some make-up exams at the midterm. So I gave him three easy questions on economics and he wrote a single sentence which had something like eight spelling mistakes in it. What's more, the sentence was nonsense. So I said to him, my dear boy, you know absolutely nothing, and that's not going to suffice. He left in a rage, saying that he didn't think that he knew nothing. So I went down to the vice-principal and said, look here, this is what our final-year student wrote. Look at all the mistakes, how can this person even take the leaving exam. She said to me, you're not here to grade his Czech, you're here to test his knowledge of economics. I don't even know what to say to that. That's just how those kind of schools work. I see nothing, I hear nothing... it's all about money.

(Mrs. Kučerová, Linden School, qualified to teach first-level students and andragogy, ca. 39 years old).

All of these experiences give teachers the feeling that the level of education on the whole is going down. The children know that they'll pass the entering exams since there are few applications, and therefore there's no reason for them to study hard. Parents are mainly concerned that their children get good grades, and don't keep track anymore whether or not these grades truly correspond to the level of knowledge that students used to achieve. The pressure for success that can be measured by an adjusted secondary-school education devalues that true value of education. Teachers feel that this isn't just a problem of the Chestnut or Linden schools, but with the system as a whole, and that they are powerless to change.

> I had a class of twenty kids, of which two went into vocational training – one as a plumber and the other as an apprentice to be a cook or waiter. All the others went on to secondary school, and that's awful. I had, for instance, one girl in the class who was always getting Ds and Fs and so she went to hairdressing school. But then I received the message: Say hello to Mrs. Brožová and tell her that I'm taking my leaving exam. I was in shock. On the one hand, you've got smart kids and then you've got kids with Ds and Fs. I'm not saying that they won't make their way. They'll make their way, and I told their parents that the boy training to be a plumber would be much better off than the kid whose parents find him some school where he can pass the leaving exam, or the boy with the F at midterm but who gets into secondary school.
>
> (Mrs. Veberová, Chestnut School; qualified to teach Russian and Czech, also teaches German; ca. 58 years old).

Teachers aren't bothered by the fact that most of the kids get into secondary school. Rather, they feel it is unjust that the leaving exam is passed by students whose results do not meet the requirements that a true graduate should have. A diploma can be bought, and therefore it is no longer proof of obtaining a certain level.

The results of these changes are in the teachers' eyes alarming since they point to a deficiency in the system that, as individuals, they can do nothing about. Some teachers would therefore welcome a return to centralized curricula, though they admit that at present it would mean that hundreds of hours of work by individuals and entire groups of teachers would have been wasted, which would not bring about any positive change. Yet it would help if the curricula at least clearly defined the level that should be obtained at the end of each year.

The uncertainty regarding the curricula is also magnified by the insecurity that education has become a political matter and that whoever takes the helm of the ministry of education fundamentally changes something. The entire system teeters, and any change is viewed by teachers with a certain dose of distrust. The Linden principal described the situation in these terms:

> Each year we sit down and plan what we'll do that year and what we'll do over the course of two and three years, and the worst thing is that, due to all

this, we have to keep changing our plans. It's as if you're in a boat heading for shore and islands keep appearing that you have to avoid. And you can't go straight. You have to keep avoiding those who throw all the administrative tasks at you, trying to trip you up. The thing is, the path could be easy and direct. All those little islands in your way are so unnecessary.

(Mr. Řehák, current Linden principal; qualified to teach geography and Russian; ca. 50 years of age)

The changes in society and in education correlate to changes that are reflected by teachers and the various individuals involved. Teachers, as well as parents and students, have changed. Their overall living conditions have changed, and this has had a major impact on their relations.

Kids and parents have changed

It's clear that teachers perceive the social changes through the prism of their day-to-day lives at schools with kids and their parents. They speak a lot about both groups. At Chestnut, teachers speak more about the kids and only then about the parents, while at Linden the parents are more frequently discussed than the children. Yet in analyzing the situation and explaining it, the teachers at both schools largely share the same views on these topics.

In the case of the **children**, the teachers are clear about two things. They believe that every older generation always "complains" about the young, so the overall sentiment that kids are worse today than they used to be needs to be relativized. On the other hand, the teachers feel that the social changes in combination with the arrival of new technology and today's rapidly transforming world have created a unique situation that has strongly impacted their relations with the kids.

In the interviews the teachers contemplated in what way today's children are different than before. In their eyes the changes in kids are the results of social changes embedded in the backdrop of the ongoing school reform. All respondents, regardless of age, gender or taught subject, agree in what ways kids have changed compared to previous students.

The teachers perceive the changes in kids on the same scale as society as a whole – more freedom – too much freedom. In their view, the kids are much more independent, expect a partnership approach, know their rights, can communicate better and are more used to being partners than subordinates. In comparison with the previous period when kids were fearful, today's kids aren't as scared. This is also confirmed by the town mayor, who contributed to setting up a children's council, and is nicely surprised that the kids know how to get involved and come up with so many good ideas.

But there is also another side of this. Though the kids know their rights, they seem to have less of a grasp on their responsibilities. They are more "assertive," but they often don't know their boundaries and are ruder – these are just a few statements that repeatedly came up. Yet the teachers also responded with a dose of humor in asking to what extent their view is determined by their age and thus normal over a lifetime. Despite their willingness to relativize the situations, it was clear that there was genuine concern of whether our society was taking the right path.

> But then, I don't know if isn't just our age. Perhaps if I were fifteen years younger, I'd see things differently. I think that I could take a lot more before, because it didn't even occur to me that I have to give the kid the best possible example. Then as life passes, you realize that the example has to come from you and you have to know how to act since they have to know that they will too someday have to.
>
> (Mrs. Okázalová, Linden School, approbation history, ca. 42 years of age)

Aware that they are relativizing, the teachers agree that greater freedom for children often results in too much or even uncontrollable freedom. This is obviously problematic for the teachers and they are trying to understand how it occurred.

Some teachers, who spent their entire life in a city or small town, mainly see the difference in the environmental influence. One respondent who taught in a Prague school even spoke of kids from the villages as "Bullerby kids." They jump on the trampoline and have a childhood. They laugh and know how to play. However, one representative of the older generation added that, compared with how the world used to be, today's kids have stopped playing. They have mainly witnessed that over the past eight years and say that we have actually taken away their childhood. The world is fast and loud, and the children are too. They blast their MP3s; they themselves scream and don't know how to listen, and they don't know how to wait until another has finished expressing his or her opinion. The respondents see this as a direct consequence of adult influence.

It was clear during the interviews that the teachers are troubled by the kids' behavior. During one interview at Chestnut School, I asked the respondent to explain precisely the difficulties in relating to the kids. The teacher thought about it a while and then recounted a recent story. The teacher was monitoring the corridor when two girls, some three meters away from her, were talking loudly so that the teacher could hear. One of the girls said to the other: "Look at what that fleabag is wearing today." As the interviewer, I was slightly taken aback by this. I was familiar with this school, and I was surprised to hear of such an incident there. It was completely at odds with what I had at one time been able to imagine in the milieu. The teacher continued, saying it was difficult since she didn't know how to react – whether to respond or to pretend as if she didn't hear it. I asked how often such situations occurred. She answered that such incidences were common, and that it was the teachers' daily bread.

Following that specific interview, I began to ask other respondents to talk about kids' worsened, uninhibited behavior. Here are two examples:

Sometimes... I usually get along with them, but then there are kids who are explicitly against you, and now that collective wants to get under your skin, and even scraped my colleague's car. One of the students just took a coin and scraped her car. The kids really have changed, and I think it's happened recently.

(Mrs. Veberová, Chestnut School; qualified to teach Russian and Czech, also teaches German; ca. 58 years old).

You have ignoramuses in your class... He sits there and takes out a poker set and begins to play with the chips. Well, I was there explaining the math and, thank god, we've only got one problematic student in the class. So he starts playing with the poker set. And I tell him that he should realize that math is a skill he would need no matter what job he does. But he doesn't care.

(Mrs. Krečmerová, Chestnut School; studied to be a Czech language and art teacher, today teaches English; 51 years old).

In addition to such distinct occurrences such as playing poker during the lesson, the teachers often mentioned the permanent presence of vulgarisms in students' communication with them. The kids even send their teachers inappropriate text messages, etc. Mrs. Bílková – a teacher representing the younger generation – said that when she was a student teachers would not have allowed the kind of behavior that students exhibit toward teachers today.

Teachers perceive these changes as a direct result of changes in society.

They're shallow. They just quickly finish something and then go on to something else. Or if I compare them to past students in creating something, students used to do things more carefully. Today's kids aren't interested in anything, they just want to finish it no matter the result. The most important thing for them is that they somehow complete the task. It doesn't matter to them if it's a good job. They just care that it's done and they can go on to something else.

(Mr. Šlosarová, Chestnut School; qualified to teach history and art; ca. 47 years old)

According to the teachers, problems with kids are completely independent of the teaching method used or of the content of the curriculum that they try to impart to them.

Yet aside from these pessimistic responses, there are also teachers who instead feel that the kids are very friendly – such as Mrs. Poláková. She does allow, however, that this could also be because she only teaches part-time at the school and does not have to be with the kids all the time. As an external worker she can enjoy teaching and apparently shares a lot of laughs with the kids.

There are also great differences between the individual classes and individual students at the schools. Bullying has, for instance, occurred in one class at Chestnut, and another class at that school is very problematic as a whole due to its makeup (student-athletes with a predominance of boys). Teachers from Linden also mention similar differences between the classes.

The mutual relations among the kids are, in the teachers' eyes, increasingly influenced by the social situation of the individual families. The teachers do not feel that this is a crucial matter, but they do know of classes in which some kids insult others for coming from a lower-class environment. The level of wealth of the individual families influences how the kids choose friends – "I'm not going to be your friend because you're poor." Some kids vacation at the sea twice a year, some none at all. The question of family class used to be only apparent in secondary school, but now it has shifted to also include primary school. Now, for instance, girls in primary school make fun of others for the brand of clothing they wear.

But this issue of social differences also depends on the class in question. In some classes it doesn't play a primary role, in other classes relations amongst kids are strongly dictated by these social differences.

I have a boy in my class who comes to school in normal clothes. It's not as if he's dirty or neglected, or anything like that. He has a very nice mother, who is always there for him if he needs her. And yet… He's quickly the target of all laughter. He's very nice and I think that it took us a long time before we got him into a position in which the class or at least some of the kids in the class, understood that it doesn't matter what you wear, but that they had to go deeper if they wanted to know the kid. I felt like it was going to be alright. But then everything began to come apart at the seams in the seventh grade. Everyone was insulting him; it was really bad. So I sat down with Mrs. Vybíralová to discuss what to do. We then came up with community groups. In these groups we discussed situations and tried to resolve problematic relations amongst kids. When he got to the eighth grade I felt that things had settled down and that it was better. But then this year – in the ninth grade at the Christmas party – the boys tried to be funny and so they gave him the biggest present and inside was SOMETHING [she indicates excrement – author's note]. He was sitting next to me, so I told him just to take the present to the back, not to unwrap it, which upset the boys since they had been looking forward to it being opened. Then they stopped since the holidays were upon us. We then discussed it with an advisor, and after the holidays we talked about it with the boys individually, and since then they've left him alone. But that was just because it was in January and they were worried that we would give them some kind of punishment.

(Mrs. Okázalová, Linden School, qualified to teach history, ca. 42 years of age)

According to the teacher, the kids are also "hungry for contact" and that might be why the kids' situation bothers them so much. Teachers do not view them as the aggressors, but more as victims caught up in the transformation and having paid dearly for it. They lost their genuine and deep relationship with their parents and then even amongst themselves. The superficiality has deeper roots than the lazy indifference of a socially and emotionally saturated individual.

They also have that armor. To reach them you have to penetrate it. Because few will tell you it, since they have completely different problems, or are in love or… Something always slips out of them, and you can deduce from that.

I think that for the most part their parents are wrapped up in their own worlds and no longer have much time for these kids. Not even for the younger ones it seems.

(Mrs. Krečmerová, Chestnut School; qualified to teach Czech language and art; today teaches English, 51 years old).

Teachers react in different ways to the kid's desire for contact. At any rate, it's clear from their responses that the changes in the kids also alter the demands on teachers and results in new dilemmas. They face a combination of the kids needing contact and possessing a higher level of vulgarity, while the kids also behave with less restraint towards the teachers. The kids feel as if they are the teachers' equals and use vulgar expressions in their communication with them.

Meanwhile, the teachers feel somewhat at a loss. Some mention that "one disciplinary measure" would often fix it, though this is no longer allowed. The authoritative style stands in contrast to the liberal and friendly approach to students. Here too there is much uncertainty among the teachers as to what is actually correct and how they should react in certain situations. This tension amongst teaching styles then produces tension in the teachers' mutual relationships.

> I think that those kinds of authoritative teachers don't discuss much with the kids. They give the kids the work and that's it. They don't hear the kids' opinions. Maybe they simply don't want to have discussions with them; it makes things harder for them, more work. Their attitude is that they've done their work and that's all there is, but I don't think there are that many teachers like that. But a lot of them... Well, I don't know. Maybe I'm overly friendly, but I also know how to maintain authority. They certainly listen to me. Recently we were two teachers with forty kids in Dresden. I wasn't worried. I knew that they would do what I said.
>
> (Mrs. Bílková, Chestnut School; originally a social worker, today teaches geography, natural history and informatics; ca. 35 years old).

At Linden, the teachers believe that good relations are fundamental for coping with difficult situations. Principal Řehák feels similarly and says that his goal is "satisfied kids, satisfied parents and satisfied teachers." At any rate, the teachers spend a lot of time thinking about their students, trying to come up with their own answer to the question of what kids at the basic school should learn in terms of relationships.

> I think it's important that they are grounded in those traditional values. Like the ten commandments. If one has that kind of formed personality, it doesn't matter if he is left or right oriented. Because which is it better to be? The right which crushes everything or the left which went nuts and wanted to share everything? Obviously, it will lead to a compromise; it can't happen without opposition. So here the people have to be one kind or the other.

I personally feel that the most educational moment in the class is when an argument occurs. An argument that doesn't get out of hand. Those children learn to argue. And learn to listen to their opponent. The thing is to let things naturally develop in the class even if it leads to an argument, to keep it under control and force the kids to think about it. I feel that the class is a kind of a small model of society. There are ambitious kids there, and you recognize the kid of ambitious parents. That kid brings candy for everyone and is able to share. Then there are kids who are indifferent, and kids that are timorous and kids who are ambitious. It's simply a cross-section of society.

(Mrs. Hartová, Linden School, qualified to teach first-level students and special education, 57 years old).

The relatively harmonious image of relationships between teachers and children in which both sides try to seek a common path through the new age is disturbed by several dramatic situations. In some cases, the kids' bad behavior even led to teachers opting for early retirement and to a feeling of absolute exhaustion and frustration.

Exhaustion as a reason for early retirement was mentioned by several teachers, including Mrs. Grosmanová. I asked her to recall one symbolic moment that would characterize her disillusionment:

Actually there was one moment, but it was already too late. I came into class intent on checking homework. Of the thirty kids in the class, two had their homework. Or there's some work that's based on the homework. From the reading, for instance. So it ruins your whole class. You basically have no leverage, so don't think you do. After that I no longer really cared. Well, I cared, but I was more like, you don't want to do your homework, so don't. I was no longer able to check it, or mark who had done it or not... If only two kids out of the whole class do their homework then you spend at least five minutes marking down who doesn't have it. And one time I came to class and saw written on the blackboard "Mrs. Grossmanová is a twat." That was the moment. That was the breaking point for me. I stopped coming to work and stayed home for two months. I mean, I know that kids say things about teachers. But to have it written like that. I'd never come across anything like that before and it was the straw that broke the camel's back.

(Mrs. Grosmanová, Linden School, qualified to teach Czech language, history, currently retired, ca. 58 years old)

In this context the teacher's emphasis on the kids' discipline seems like a reaction to their frustration from the increasingly rude behavior in schools. Discipline would help teachers control this kind of borderline situation, yet it is this very discipline that has been devalued in schools. The teachers don't feel that discipline should be blind obedience, but see it more as respect for established rules and appropriate behavior.

Homework can serve as an example. Teachers often have to deal with kids showing up to class without their homework. Since the teaching plan depends on the kids having done their homework and only two of thirty bring it, a problem obviously arises. Inconsistency in doing homework can then in some cases be linked to inconsistencies in the school, and the entire system begins to fall apart. One of the teachers interviewed who also taught at another school recalled having a problematic student in her class who would always arrive late to class. The principal kept promising to meet with his parents but he never did. Then gradually other students joined him in coming late. That was one of the reasons why the teacher began to look for a position with another school.

It's clear that the teachers often wonder whether a liberal educational style based on friendly relations to the kids and a project method of teaching is compatible with the basic requirement of discipline and consistency in human relationships. During the research, several teachers cited Comenius's words: "a school without discipline is like a mill without water." The question is, what would Comenius say today?

The teachers are unsure where things went wrong. The contradiction between their view that a school really doesn't work without discipline, and their belief that they're the only ones who insist on discipline is apparent. In the matter of discipline, the teachers' personal convictions clash with how in their view the world outside schools regards discipline. The teachers see it as a prerequisite for a smooth teaching process, while they feel that outside schools it is viewed more as an obstacle, like the useless residue of the past.

The teachers clearly agree that the key for understanding today's situation with kids lies in the change in the Czech family. According to the teachers, the situation in families has undergone a deep transformation that has also impacted kids. Instead of blaming parents, the teachers see them more as the victims. The **parents** are, in the teachers' eyes, in a pinch. Along with demanding work and commuting, they have to raise their kids, which they have the least amount of time for. In a society based on ambition, pressure for success and a fast tempo, parents are supposed to be good in all areas. But this is impossible. The criteria for "being a good parent" are debatable. Every parent has a different approach and the tenacious attempt of parents to obtain the new ideal does not result in a quality life. The teachers feel that this basic diagnosis has many symptoms that are apparent in schools.

The relation between teachers and parents exists on several levels. 1) Teachers judge how children are raised at home by how they act in school. 2) Teachers and parents are also in direct contact, motivated by the attempt to resolve a problem. 3) Regularly planned contact between parents and teachers occurs at parent-teacher meetings and at other possible school events.

Since relations between teachers and parents go through dramatic changes that are apparent on many levels, we need to take examine the individual levels of the relations separately:

1) Teachers base their judgements on how kids are raised at home by how they act at home.

Teachers mention a broad range of situations in which kids act unusually at school. Upon closer examination, the teachers ascertain that the kids learn these traits at home. An inability to concentrate during the lesson can be caused by the kid being hungry, since the morning rush prevented him or her from eating and the parent forgot to pack him a snack. Kids don't eat the meals served in the school cafeteria because they're unfamiliar with them, not having homemade meals at home and only frozen foods heated up in the microwave oven. These situations are difficult enough to resolve, but then teachers are supposed to lead the children in a different direction and talk about other things, which give these situations a more dramatic charge.

> Well, health class for one. What am I supposed to do when we read about vitamins in class. And the kids bring schnitzel every Monday from home. Well, that kind of family and school, at least in those villages, they're stuck in a rut.
>
> (Mrs. Grosmanová, Linden School; qualified to teach Czech language and history; currently retired, ca. 56 years old)

The degree to which the kids are prepared for school at home has nothing to do with how well off a family is financially:

> These parents drive their kids to school in the fanciest cars but the kids don't have anything with them, no pencil, nothing. And these kids are not from poorer families. The parents just don't give a damn about the kids. They're just not that important for the parents. I see it firsthand. Last year I met with parents who had four boys, four kids, and those kids didn't have anything, not even notebooks. It was clear that they weren't getting enough care. Though

the parents aren't educated, they're able to make money. They work for some dispatching company, and drive up in a nice car, a Citroën 607, and that's not a cheap car. It's clear that the family has no problems making ends meet, but their values are elsewhere. The kids are completely neglected. They're in the eighth grade and their vocabulary is pitiful; they just sit at the computer.

(Mrs. Hanzelová, Linden School, qualified to teach Japanese studies, has an international certificate in English, the minimal level for teaching; ca. 44 years of age).

The teachers feel that not enough attention is being paid to raising the kids at home, which is apparent in things that the teachers consider to be elementary, such as the kids reacting to being told something, or listening to basic instructions.

All it takes is a little effort in raising them, having them say thank you a few time, or everyday things like reacting to a request the first time it is made. They're used to their parents asking them ten times before they react. But if you ask them to sit down, it's not as if they'll automatically do it. And that's absolutely fundamental. At first this really, I don't want to say threw me for a loop, but I found it strange. If I hadn't obeyed at home, there would have been hell to pay. And the way they act toward their parents, how they speak to them, for instance on the phone, when I overhear their conversation.

(Mrs. Bílková, Chestnut School; originally a social worker, today teaches geography, natural history and informatics; ca. 35 years old).

2) Parent-teacher meetings during the school year to resolve discipline matters.

According to the teachers, the most important point for a successful upbringing in the family is building a real emotional background. And the teachers feel that the parents don't have time for that. The number of children from divorced parents and broken homes has dramatically increased in schools. Teachers believe that this too is a certain destabilization of the entire system. And that it's obviously related to the values and example that the parents provide for their kids. It doesn't even have to be a major turning point like a divorce. Sometimes it's enough how parents speak to their kids:

I'll give an example. One time I was speaking with a student's mother and I said: Your Magda is such a pleasant and nice girl, and yet she talks like a sailor. And the mother said: "What a stupid cow." So it was clear to me. I'm not going to have an effect here. Ethical behavior has deteriorated everywhere.

(Mrs. Slavíčková, Linden School; qualified to teach history; ca. 70 years of age)

The teachers see great differences in the upbringing of children and their children. Some parents make an effort, but others are actually leading their children down the wrong path and this leaves teachers with a feeling of helplessness. The values that the children bring with them from home to school largely create a school's environment. In some places it is very positive, but in others the parents' value system is practically in contradiction with the law:

I met for instance with a father whose son had racist inclinations. The father told me just between the two of us: "I'm a racist, it's just the way I am. I hate gypsies and I'm not going to raise my boy any other way." So the teacher really isn't able to do anything. Then the kid often acts hypocritically. He acts in a certain way just to comply.

(Mrs. Hloušková, current vice-principal at Chestnut School; qualified to teach geography, ca. 59 years old).

When a problem arises, the teachers have the feeling that the parents are more prone than before to hastily blame the school. Usually the parents reject the idea that the problem arose at home. The teachers feel that the reason for this is that, due to the parents' work load, they don't have enough time to properly raise their kids and this easily leads to their search for a culprit outside the family.

In comparison to the previous status quo, the parents have obtained greater power and are more aware of their authority. Moreover, they are now more inclined to complain about teachers, and in some cases even had teachers punished.

I simply drew the mother's attention to the fact that her daughter was smoking. And that she had even offered a teacher a cigarette and that she carries them in her pockets. Well, the mother started in on me that the girl had told her… that I had marked it in the class book and requested a meeting. So the meeting was set and the mother came and when I told her she said, no, my daughter told me that she doesn't smoke, that she doesn't have any cigarettes, that she didn't offer any cigarettes to another teacher. I said, look here, I didn't make this up. I'm not the kind to make something up, I just thought you might want to keep an eye on her... It wasn't pretty. She went berserk on me, yelling that she would put her kid in a different school. I told her that was within her rights. You commute to Lán where you work, there are plenty of schools there, put her in one of them, I calmly told her, look here, it will be the best for both of us. I'll have peace of mind, she'll be your problem and you'll be able to do with her what you want... Less than two weeks had gone by when the vice-principal told me that a complaint had been filed against me. In no way did I talk coarsely or vulgarly with the mother, nor did I yell at her in the hallway... I said, look here, I've several witnesses who were present during the exchange and they can come say how it really was. In the end, the vice-principal admitted that the mother was probably over exaggerating.

(Mr. Brož, Chestnut School, qualified to teach chemistry, workshops, ca. 67 years old)

In that case the teacher did not end up with any penalty, but it could have turned out differently. The teachers recall various situations in which parents opposed them with such force that they opted to leave the school or were even fired.

3) Regular planned contact during the year
During the school year the teachers notice greater variety in the parents' attitude toward the school. On the one hand the parents are more interested – they've read the curriculum and keep an eye on whether the teachers stick to it. On the other hand, some parents show less interest in reacting to the various messages from the school, to notes and to requests to communicate.

At both observed schools the class meetings are an important subject, though each has a different take on the meetings. At Chestnut the teachers more or less feel that parents only sporadically attend class meetings, and also communicate less with the school.

At Linden, they notice a similar trend, though it is not as apparent and the teachers themselves took the initiative to come up with ideas how to organize the class meetings in various ways and to attract the attention and interest of parents.

Take the parent-teacher meetings. They're able to talk to you differently there. Not just about school. We also discuss the kids' interests, what they do after school... we started with the sixth form to change the parent-teacher meetings so they weren't sitting in rows at the desks. Instead, I had the kids make a circle with chairs and we bought little cakes and made coffee and tea... Those school desks, they'd sit there and have the feeling that they had to sit up straight and follow the rules, so now they're beginning to get over that and I think even the relationship is a little different. They've begun to ask about that which they would have normally kept to themselves. Even outside the meetings they're more at ease in communicating. So that relationship is a little different. And I for one am glad that parents are becoming more communicative. I think it's worth it. But there has to be a boundary on how far they can go. On the other hand, the parents couldn't care less about the board of education...

(Mrs. Okázalová, Linden School; qualified to teach history; ca. 42 years of age)

At Linden they are trying to improve communication with parents in still another way. A few years ago the school introduced a questionnaire to gauge the satisfaction of parents and students with the school environment. This enables the situation in general to be monitored and provides school management with information on how parents and students feel at the school.

Despite these examples of minor successes in communication between parents and the school, the teachers feel that the parents' relation to the school has changed in recent years and the teachers are trying to understand this change. Some respondents speak of the change in the very perception of family–school relations since the time they themselves were parents of kids going to school.

The teacher Mrs. Okázalová believes that parents often see the school as a coercive institution and feel they have to take the side of their children. The question is obviously to what extent this is caused by the parents' prior experiences. Many of them had experiences with totalitarian-type schools and perhaps still lack faith in the system. This hypothesis was among the reasons for the ensuing discussions with parents. The fluctuating relations between school and family is demonstrated by the following example:

In the 6th grade a boy was caught lying three times for some reason, so I told his mother that he was lying in school, and when I told her the example, she said: "That kind of thing goes on all the time in school." I have to admit that I was speechless and had no idea how to respond to that. Obviously the parents see one kind of behavior at home and refuse to believe that their sweet child can act differently at school. That's the worst when you're arguing with parents who refuse to believe how it really is. I understand that parents are parents, and that they're going to defend their child under all circumstances, but a little objectivity wouldn't hurt. Maybe the problems that they have now could have been avoided. Because now their kid is growing bigger than them.

(Mrs. Bílková, Chestnut School; originally a social worker, today teaches geography, natural history and informatics; ca. 35 years old).

One of the reasons why relations between the school and parents are sometimes rocky is, once again, the pressure to perform. Parents want their children to have good marks and guaranteed success in society. The teachers are the ones who give out the marks. The relationship between teacher, school and student is then limited to obtaining the maximum effect with minimum effort, and this can cause great problems, and even more so if the two sides have differing opinions on what the child should learn and how he or she should learn it in school.

There were cases at both schools in which teachers had to leave the school due to the direct intervention of parents. Respondents from Linden spoke of a specific conflict at the other school. The parents formed an alliance against one of the teachers and she was forced at the end of the school year, in which the research was conducted, to retire prematurely. She was one of two teachers who had refused to give an interview at the start of that same year, claiming to have neither the desire nor the strength to talk about school after her teaching day. This occurred at a time when Chestnut was forced to let go of one teacher each year due to a lack of students, and the principal decided to let go of the teacher whom the parents had opposed.

And what do the parents think?

It became clear during the research that the teachers and parents underwent a fundamental change that symbolically represents value changes in society at large and reflects certain contradictions in values. I therefore decided to invite parents from both schools to respond to my questions at parent-teacher meetings.

Even though this consisted of a brief exchange within the framework of several individual interviews at Chestnut and a half-hour meeting with a group of parents at Linden, we can glean from these talks a more comprehensive view of the previously examined topics.

I was invited to a class at Linden where the meetings were organized in a slightly different way. The parents were seated around a large table in the middle of the classroom; the students and teacher had baked a cake in the afternoon, made coffee and tea, and, after the meetings commenced, the students went out into the hallway where they waited for their parents.

Since there were many more parents willing to talk to me from Linden than from Chestnut, I will in this part draw more from their perceptions, while also drawing from the interviews at Chestnut.

The group discussions were undertaken in several phases, and it became clear from them that behavior and discipline are important for both teachers and parents. The discussion about this was the most turbulent part of the meeting. The talks about discipline was mostly initiated by the parents. I merely asked at the start what had changed in education from the time the parents themselves had gone to school and then began to inquire in more detail about the content of the lessons and methods. However, the parents quickly interrupted me and began to speak about discipline and respect. I heard: "You can't learn anything without respect," "we were better listeners than our children." According to the parents, a school should instill discipline in the kids. In their view, students are much less disciplined than they used to be. I asked the parents who should be in charge of instilling the discipline. The parents began to criticize themselves. "We're all rushing about between kids and work," "It's not the kids' fault, it's that we don't have enough time for them." Parents and teachers agreed that the hustle bustle between work and family is detrimental to their relationship with their kids. Parents would like to devote more time to their kids, they just don't know when to do it and how to handle it. They would appreciate it if they didn't face the task alone. "Our parents would beat us," the parents laughed when recollecting how they were made to show respect as kids. One view frequently voiced was whether "a single disciplinary measure" wouldn't be more effective in some cases than constant haranguing and conduct marks.

Parents also mentioned that a turning point occurs in conduct during the second level, when the influence of friends increases and kids spend more time unmonitored on the streets. It was previously common that when kids misbehaved on the streets, somebody would admonish them. Society's supervision was, according to parents, greater. Such admonishing no longer occurs, and since parents are at work – often far from the home – they often have no idea of what their kids get up to.

I asked the parents how often they discussed the subject of discipline with their kids at home. One mother openly admitted: "I'm afraid that if I bring it up, my kid will stop coming home." Other parents nodded in agreement. Parents are apparently afraid that if they increase disciplinary pressure, they might lose their kids.

New media and computer technology obviously also effect the overall situation. Some parents feel that their kids spend more time on their computers than they should; others feel that they still have the situation under control. One respondent also mentioned that the school too quickly and readily accepted the existence of new media and the Internet. Older kids in the secondary school get homework they have to do using the internet – so the family needs to have an Internet connection at home. This respondent felt that it would greatly help if, for instance, two variations of the homework were assigned: one with and one without use of the Internet.

It was on this subject that I asked whether and how often their kids were reading books. Five respondents raised their hands and said that they felt that their kids were reading enough; others felt that their kids were only reading a little. There were only a few parents who believed that their kids were reading very rarely or not at all.

Parents feel that **differences in a family's social status** impact relationships between children, but not to a greater degree than when they were children. In pre-1989 times, some children had, for instance, things from the state-run foreign currency shop Tuzex, so the situation was similar to now. At any rate, parents don't feel as if they're under great pressure in this regard. A family's economic situation is instead influenced by the change in the number of trips and activities organized by the school, all of which cost money. If a family has two or three kids in school, the expenses related to these school activities really start to add up.

The respondents rate **relations among kids** as essentially good, not differing much from the parents' memories of their school days. The exception was one mother who was shocked by what her daughter went through after moving from Moravia. In her view, today's kids aren't used to accepting someone new, someone different. The rivalry among children is greater and they don't work well as a group. Her daughter essentially cried the entire school year before she managed to slightly become part of the class.

The parents themselves do not maintain any mutual relations outside the school.

In the class it was clear by where they sat that they wanted to be next to someone they knew, but no families from either of the schools spend free time together.

When parents compared the **contents of the curriculum**, there was one topic that they perceived differently than the teachers. While the teachers felt that today's children learn less than their parents, the parent feel that, on the contrary, today's curriculum places much greater demands on the kids. The textbooks have changed too and parents feel that the new ones are not clearly structured and harder to work with.

Parents do feel, however, that relations between teachers and parents have changed for the better. Parents at both schools praised both teachers and the school environment on a whole as being very open. Parents believe that teachers care about their kids, that they find something good in each of them and try to sincerely and earnestly communicate with the parents about the kids. Parents feel that this certainly was not the case in the past.

The parents at both schools differed in their emphasis on **what the school should actually do.** While all parents at Chestnut said that that school should above all teach kids and guide them towards future gainful employment, the parents at Linden felt it important for the school to both educate the kids and raise them. The parents don't feel stress from their kids' marks, but since their kids spend so much time at school, they feel it important that the school also pedagogically guide their offspring.

And what do the children think?
The questionnaires for children were more a supplemental method within the framework of the overall research. The aim was to broadly characterize through the students' eye the environment that I had been analyzing for two years with the teachers. I used the questionnaire based on Higgins – Sadh research (1998) for this purpose.

The questionnaire is composed of simple statements (e.g.: students often act fairly and with respect towards one another; students help each other even if they aren't friends, etc.). Students had the following responses to choose from:

Don't agree – Rather disagree – Rather agree – Agree.

I received thirty-one completed questionnaires (16 girls and 15 boys) from Chestnut, whereas roughly half of the kids were in the 9th grade (14–15 years old) and the second half were in the sixth grade (12–13 years).

At Linden I only managed to get questionnaires from kids from the class in which the parent-teacher meetings were held. In total I received 12 completed questionnaires (9 girls and 3 boys).

It is clear from the questionnaires that the kids at Chestnut view their relations with teachers in a very positive light. They trust each other and can openly discuss things. The kids feel that the teachers are interested in them and try to work together to formulate the rules of the game. In this regard, the boys are a little more skeptical than the girls, with the former assessing their relations to teachers less positively (the response "rather agree" prevails over "agree").

Boys and girls agreed that mutual relations between kids are slightly more complex to assess. According to the kids, stealing, cheating, drug use, vandalism and playing hooky occur at the school – girls feel the situation is more critical than boys. Neither teachers nor parents mentioned any of these problems. The question is obviously whether they really don't know about these things or whether they simply didn't mention them during the research. At any rate, the kids mentioned the presence of drugs at school as the first problem.

The situation is similar at Linden – relations between children and teachers are assessed better than those solely among children. The main difference from Chestnut is that at Linden the kids said that drugs and alcohol are not used at the school and that verbal abuse and the humiliation of others does not occur.

Even though this was just one minor probe into the world of the kids at both schools, the students are essentially confirming what the teachers and parents said. The teachers basically see the kids in a positive light and it is apparent from the questionnaires that the problem from the cultural standpoint occurs more in relations among kids, which the parents also said.

Teachers after the hangover

After examining external circumstances and ascertaining how teachers see themselves, we surprisingly find that not much has changed from the teachers' perspective, that this inertia occurs on many levels, including in the school culture and relations. Let's take a look at teachers through their own eyes and re-examine the various topics.

During the interviews I asked teachers what had changed and what hadn't changed during their years in education. It's probably good to start with this, though I should emphasize that there were not any significant differences between the two schools. Many teachers feel that there haven't been any fundamental changes. In summarizing their assessment of the overall situation, it seems that there remains a significant gap between the central level, represented by the Ministry of Education, and the individual schools. The teachers call this gap non-conceptuality:

I have 28 years' experience in education. Over that period there have been fourteen ministers of education and dozens of attempts at establishing a concept for education. Yet this concept never developed into a sensible conclusion. It started with the sets method, then there were the school educational programs opened with great pomp. Now they are finding out that they're not as good as they thought they would be, and so sooner or later we'll go back to those syllabi and green books and programs for primary schools. They're all just attempts and there is a complete lack of concept. So now where is the problem. The problem isn't on our side, on the side of the executor; the problem must be with the ministry of education. The head of the fish stinks. If they're going to change ministers like socks, there is no chance that the concept can be developed into a sensible plan. No way.

(Mr. Řehák, the current principal of Linden school; qualified to teach geography and Russian; ca. 50 years of age)

What's more, the non-conceptuality is accompanied by instructions from the government: "There were orders before and now there are orders. They were useless before and now they are useless... there are still no results." Education has always been treated like Cinderella and it doesn't look to change anytime soon.

However, the teachers do feel that it's good news that relations between teachers and kids and the interest of the kids has not changed. These two constants remain typical for schools and no regime has altered that. At least some of the kids are and have always been focused, passionate and interested, and they are for teachers the main motivation for remaining in education. Some teachers dryly acknowledged that the fact that education has traditionally been on the periphery of public interest has its advantages. Indeed, only those who really want to teach and truly like kids remain in education. Otherwise, they would work in some other field. Many teachers expressed their positive relation to children and working with them during the interviews, and at times it was clear that they were speaking about something that genuinely interested them and something that they enjoyed thinking about.

Yet when they were asked to consider their position, they dryly stated that now that social status is closely linked to how much money you make and that teachers are relatively poorly paid, they feel that their status is poor.

Most people who remained in teaching did so because they enjoy what they do, and not for financial reasons. So actually I would see it more as a plus that we're poorly paid [she laughs]. Because if you're looking to make money, you're not going to go into teaching. People teach because they enjoy it. I'm not saying that those who remain in teaching wouldn't be able to do something else. That's not what I mean.

But speaking for myself, I really don't see major changes, at least around me.

(Mrs. Hloušková, current vice-principal at Chestnut School, qualified to teach geography, ca. 59 years old).

Teachers don't even notice changes in the background of their work. The bureaucracy hasn't decreased, even though less of it was promised in 1989. Another thing is that the preparation of future teachers at universities does not correspond in its quality to the requirements that teachers have and the requirements imposed on them in performing their work.

One thing that bothered teachers prior to 1989 and that has markedly improved is the amount of time spent in meetings. The older teachers in particular noted that this was a huge relief.

Access to information and possibilities of working with it remains an inconsistent category. In general, teachers acknowledged with gratitude that they have better and freer access to information, but the way it is processed seems to be an important topic. Teachers essentially praised the easier access to information via the Internet, but also agreed that previously the textbooks were of a higher quality. Although there is currently available a greater choice of textbooks, their quality is lower and the market is full of untested textbooks. For instance, the reading chosen for children is not commensurate to their age. Teachers feel that this is caused by the attempt to include as many authors as possible that were previously banned and whose books were not available. There is no longer any regard for the age in which the kids get to know these writers. Another problem is the series of textbooks. The first might seem good, luring the school into going with it, but the following books in the series do not meet the same standards. So either the school uses these textbooks of a lower quality, or it must spend high sums on another series in hopes of finding a textbook that will maintain a high quality throughout the series. This costs both the school and society at large vast sums of money.

There were a lot of new publishers, so there are a lot of new textbooks. But they only sent one part. The first was always high quality, so the schools would buy a hundred, but then the other books in the series were poor, so they'd end up having to buy a different series. They must have wasted millions on those books, and they'd all end up in the dumpster.

(Mrs. Brožová, Chestnut School; qualified to teach Czech language; currently retired, 69 years old)

One point of interest is that only one teacher mentioned that improved access to foreign literature was among the changes. A topic worthy of its own separate research is teacher's accessibility to foreign publications and how much they feel the need to draw information from books published in languages other than Czech. Teachers also mentioned traveling as a positive consequence of the political changes.

If we were to sum up the current situation regarding relations among teachers, we could call it the "hangover after the revolution." A marked improvement was noticed only in the ideological realm: teachers are less afraid to express themselves publicly and feel that there is less pressure on them to be publicly involved. This has not, however, led to a sense of satisfaction as teachers.

As for relations, the two schools share similarities in some parameters of the situation, but differ in others. The "empty staffroom" phenomenon is a current topic at both schools. In comparison with the period prior to 1989, the staffroom is less frequented by teachers especially in connection with the extinction of old rituals and with the new arrangement of the space. For instance, the teachers at both schools resolved the issue of smoking in the staffroom. It was agreed at both schools that smoking would not be permitted in the staffroom. Smokers were then instructed to smoke outside, in rooms specifically designated for smoking and in their own offices. According to the teachers, this did not cause any considerable problems at either of the schools. Yet it is a factor contributing to the "empty staffroom" phenomenon. While in 1989 the staffroom was full, after 1989 it was less so and teachers spent less time together in general. Teachers at both schools have noticed this.

The two schools markedly differ in terms of their relationships. We will therefore take a separate look at the two schools' reasons that led to the "empty staffroom".

Changes in relations at Chestnut

Following the turbulent events of 1989, the teachers feel that relations underwent a certain transformational phase that lasted several years until they were largely normalized. By normalizing relations, I mean a situation in which teachers meet with one another and work smoothly together without a feeling of heightened tension. All teachers essentially view relations at the school prior to 1989 as better than after 1989. They used the antithesis of the empty and full staffroom to prove their point. They said that before 1989, teachers actually spent time in the staffroom, spent time together and looked forward to doing so since "it was fun".

After 1989 the collective disintegrated into smaller groups. Teachers spend their free time in their offices or in the smoking room. On the other hand, the teachers feel that their relations are more open, they're able to discuss things more and that there is less fear of expressing an opinion. Yet this openness also brings with it greater rivalry and reduces the feeling of solidarity among teachers.

Another turning point in relations occurred around 2004 when young teachers arrived at the school. Representatives of both the older and younger generations spoke of a conflict between the generations that touched upon many aspects of coexistence at the school. Although representatives of the generations demonstrated mutual respect in the interviews ("the young teachers nicely accepted me"), the generational divide of teachers is strongly perceived, as is the aspect of forming smaller groups. The younger teachers have a tendency to stick together and are viewed as "not showing respect for older teachers. They don't want any advice, have no restraint, do not concede any real problems, and are wrapped up in themselves..." etc.

Since only one representative of the younger generation took part in the interview, it is difficult to generalize their take on the conflict. However, this respondent did express her views on relations between the generations regarding teaching methods. In her view the young represent a certain chaos, while the older teachers opt for order.

> There are certainly differences, huge differences, both in the approach and in the concept of the situation, but I don't think that it's fully discussed in public that there are groups of teachers that openly say it to each other, but I feel a bit of tension here since the older teachers obviously want to do things the old way. While we younger teachers see that there was some good in the old way. But some find it harder to carry on that way. Some are very much bothered by it, though they can't say it out loud. So there's some kind of, shall we say, strife, some friction... It's mainly about teaching methods. But the result is the same that the kids don't learn anything [she laughs].
>
> (Mrs. Bílková, Chestnut School; originally a social worker, today teaches geography, natural history and informatics; ca. 35 years old).

It is interesting, however, that both Mrs. Bílková and her older colleagues mention problems with the kids' behavior and are just as uncertain in seeking ways to adapt classwork to the social situations that make their way into the school setting through the kids.

We even have intergenerational relations here [laughs]. I think that the older teachers generally have the feeling that they've been wronged. For if new trends and a certain kind of teaching are going to be initiated everywhere and there's the drive to get young teachers into schools, so that now they're adding young teachers but not old ones, then what kind of message is that? I would probably react the same way if I were one of the older teachers. Especially if I had thirty years of teaching behind me, having taught x number of kids in the way I felt was best, and then someone came along and told me that my way is obsolete, that I was doing it wrong, because the research says I should be doing it in a totally different way, and then comes along a young whippersnapper with five years of pedagogical schooling. The truth is that most studying at teaching colleges are either those impassioned and wanting to teach, or those who are unsure what they want to do. In some of our classes at the teaching college there were students who said they just wanted the degree and weren't planning on teaching. Still other said they were going to teach while they were single, but that once they got married they were going to find a job where they could make real money. But that for the time being they were just having fun. So there are fewer who are now going into teaching.

(Mrs. Bílková, Chestnut School, originally a social worker, today teaches geography, natural history and informatics, ca. 35 years old).

Surprisingly, the responses of the younger and older generation of teachers do not differ that much: all grapple with the same problems, and even use the same phrases in describing them, returning to the question of discipline and how and what kids should learn. Yet a certain tension endures between the generations.

The figure of the principal is undeniably crucial for relations at the school. Teachers view this figure in two ways at Chestnut. Though the principal does not move the school forward, he does try to act fairly to everyone and doesn't try to hinder anyone. The teachers feel that he is benevolent and gives plenty of space to his colleagues. The principal sees himself in a similar light:

I think that much depends on the school principal. If he's dramatic and insists that we act quickly, or if he's more of an idler then we need to wait, think it over and ponder its impact. Sometimes I move quickly, sometimes slowly. Sometimes it works out well, sometimes it doesn't. I think that our way is better than deciding quickly. And if we reach a point that we believe is good, well we'll get there just the same. But we'll steer clear if it's not the right thing for us, because then it's hard to go back. In our case, for instance, now there's a problem with money from the EU. Hats off to Adam [vice-prin-cipal Neuman – author's note] for getting involved. He told me that those are things that one person has to do. He took it upon himself. He prepared all the applications, completed them all, all I had to do was sign them. And now we have two and a half million. Now we have interactive boards in all the classrooms, the training is behind us, and we have our teaching aids. I don't want to praise him, but I will have to. It's wonderful. The same goes for the education program. He understands it, and doesn't mind reading those ad-ministrative things. Sometimes these things can be overly bureaucratic, the language and all... so it's great that we can get it done together. I feel as if it's working well, but someone else has to be responsible for it. That's how I feel about it; maybe someone else would see it in a completely different way.

(Mr. Hájek, the current principal of Chestnut School; qualified to teach geography and physical education; ca. 56 years of age)

Principal Hájek has very little patience for all administrative demands coming from outside the school. His motto is "have your cake and eat it too." His experience from, for instance, writing annual reports has made him feel this way. These obviously very much bother him and it's quite apparent in comparison with Linden. While Linden boasts of its results in its annual reports, the annual reports from Chestnut are characterized by a minimum of work put into them. Principal Hájek justifies this ap-proach in his belief that nobody reads them anyway. Besides the school inspector, I was the first to take an interest in them. After the inspection, the inspector apparently said that the annual report was fine, but that it had to be displayed in a visible place. Principal Hájek became incensed and placed it where he wanted. He made a copy of the first page, put it up in the hallway in front of the principal's office and left it there. Ac-cording to him, nobody has since noticed that this highly visible annual report is not complete.

This small symbolic act might indicate what Principal Hájek thinks of the current education system. According to all available information, this director has a very lax approach and is very kind in the school, which teachers appreciate about him. At the same time, the teachers have voiced the opinion that it would be good if someone else became principal after so many years, so that the school could get new stimulus.

Changes in relations at Linden
Relations at Linden School are also undergoing a certain dynamic change that can be deemed a calm after the storm. This turbulent time

was marked by the exodus of many teachers after Principal Zámečník took over. However, his stint as principal and the upheaval in the faculty was a relatively short period. At Linden the overall picture is much less dramatic and could be summed up as relations that were good before 1989 and still are. Relations are not a pressing issue at Linden.

Those who worked at the school before 1989 say that relations had always been good at the school and that the regime change had no influence on them. Teachers did not hold personal grudges and did not allow politics to enter relations. Obviously, the situation after the exodus of many teachers and the arrival of new ones was a test of the good relations. Some of those who were hired at that time recall that they were looked on in the beginning with a certain dose of mistrust, but that the situation quickly improved and relations became strong again. Respondents agree that relations are currently good, but that several topics have arisen that influence the quality and stability of relations.

The subject of social differences has slowly emerged among the teachers. Before 1989, teachers were equal even in financial terms, but this is no longer true.

> We all made the same amount, maybe communists higher up in the party made more, and those who were in the union might have received a little more. It was usually put up on the bulletin board, and we all had a husband making more or less the same. Whereas after 1989 even that changed. Husbands began business ventures, some families inherited wealth, and some people started acting differently like "There's no way I'm going to that pub, we only go to this one." I remember one colleague coming to school in September in a coat and said, "Hey, what's this? A two thousand crown bill in my pocket." Her husband was an entrepreneur and she had forgotten that she had 2,000 crowns in her pocket, which certainly could not have happened to me. And when I observe the young teachers, I realize that they don't have the same kind of collective that we had.
>
> (Mrs. Bílá, Linden School; qualified to teach math, civics, ca. 60 years old)

Teachers do spend time in the staffroom. Yes, it is emptier than it used to be, but teachers do frequent it while also having the possibility to withdraw when they need time to prepare for class or want to take a break from the "gossip" that has traditionally been a part of the staffroom. Teachers also go out together on Friday afternoon to a cafe. Though fewer may go, there's less free time these days and someone might want to go to a "classier pub", it's not a problem and those who feel like it join in.

One respondent's testimony provides us with a glimpse of where the boundary of trust lies: she speaks of what she would openly talk about with a colleague and what she wouldn't. "It's not as if I would go around boasting about whom I vote for, but on the other hand I would be fine with criticizing a politician."

For the most part, the teachers at Linden feel that they have great relations with their colleagues. They work well together and help each other. A respondent who worked at schools in Prague said that she believed that this was common for schools in small towns. Relations are not anonymous, and although people gossip about each other, they also stick together more.

The truest test of relations has always been the week-long school trip to the countryside. Teachers at Linden feel that this trip is also a rather pleasant experience. The harmonious relations are sometimes disturbed by kids acting up, but this evidently does not prevent the overall satisfaction of the school's teachers.

One more serious problem is the reaction to the Ministry of Education's requirement that unqualified teachers not work at schools beginning in 2014. Unlike Chestnut School, where none of the respondents mentioned this matter, at Linden it is much discussed. At the time of the interviews one of the teachers learned that she would have to leave the school owing to insufficient qualifications. Being in her fifties, she will have a hard time finding work. What's more, she is a very good teacher liked by the kids.

Principal Řehák also commented on the subject of qualifications. In his eyes this was one of the Ministry's understandable, though not well considered requirements. It's as if a diploma from a teacher's college could decide whether someone is a good or bad teacher. The principal discussed with teachers this requirement and dealt with it ahead of time, and many of the teachers furthered their education so that they would meet the requirements by 2014. There were, however, individuals that for various reasons – often personal – did not further their education and were forced, due to the administrative requirement, to gradually leave the school.

On the whole, there are more teachers working at Linden that originally had different teaching qualifications. They've furthered their education, but see it as purely formalistic. The teachers don't understand how, for instance, a person who has an internationally acknowledged certificate in English, is not qualified in the Ministry's eyes to teach it at a basic school. The pedagogical minimum that this respondent must reach does not in her view add in any way to what she already knows.

Forced departures add tension to otherwise harmonious relations, mainly between the teachers and principal. Otherwise relations between the principal and his or her subordinate colleagues are proper and solid, and according to all respondents it's clear that both sides strive for common satisfaction.

The school's role in society

Since during the interviews the teachers spoke a lot about social changes that influence the performance of their profession, I asked them whether they feel that expectations linked to the school had changed. In other words, what parents and society actually expect from the school and whether this expectation had changed over the course of the teachers' professional lives. The teachers were all in agreement on this point. They feel that expectations had changed considerably.

This question gets to the root of the problem that teachers feel is very deep and concerns the radical change in values that they've gone through. For teachers, it is mainly the parents who represent the expectations from society, and so we again return to relations between parents and teachers, or to the expectations of parents and to the actual possibilities of teachers.

The views of teachers are perhaps best summarized here:

I think before parents wanted a basic thing. For the school to prepare the kids in some way. Today they want the kids to be successful regardless of whether they are well prepared... And maybe that high-level of difficulty is hindering us now. Maybe that school here in the Remízek surroundings has a reputation of sorts. I've heard about it; kids from those villages, if they have a choice of whether to go to one school or another, and this isn't anything against the other school, but they say, I'm not going to Chestnut, the teachers are too demanding there and they want too much from you. That's what has changed. They avoid difficulty and take the easy way; they're interested in getting good grades and nothing more. And we're the ones who end up paying for it since schools are funded per child, per capita, and if the parents are going to look at it that way and say that they'd rather put kids in another school because it's easier, and less demanding, we'll have fewer students and less money. So it's a disadvantage to us.

(Mr. Neuman, Chestnut School; qualified to teach physical education; ca. 58 years old)

This basic observation is evident in many other aspects. The teachers feel that one radical change is that parents expect schools to both educate and raise their kids. They want both expectations to be satisfied so that it places the least possible burden on parents and their free time spent with children.

Teachers give specific reasons for their opinion regarding this matter:

The truth is that mothers used to be home more, or they worked fewer hours, and they would pick up their kids from school or the kids would go home for lunch. This is no longer the case. Now there are after-school clubs until 4:30 p.m. and the kids are there until then. A number of parents commute to Prague for work and don't get back until later. So parents work more, and have to commute to work, so they expect more services from the school since they don't have time for the kids. They have their kids here from 6:30 a.m. until 4:30 p.m. and expect the school to take care of everything. But I think that this is caused by their need to commute in order to have work. So then they expect that we'll take care of everything in raising their kids.

(Mrs. Kovářová, the current vice-principal of Linden school; qualified to teach mathematics and technology basics; ca. 48 years of age)

During the period I was conducting the research it was actually decided, upon the parents' request, that the after-school program's hours be extended.

Parents actually react in two ways to this basic living situation of families. One group of parents "leave everything up to the kids," and don't want to deal with anything. The other group tries to be overly involved, wanting to know exactly what is happening in school, why a teacher does something one way and not another. One of the reasons that this discussion is even possible is that the centralized curricula were done away with, allowing for greater freedom and thus more possibilities of choice. A question that arises in comparison with the past situation is who can influence what happens in schools and to what extent.

What's more, parents' expectations are considerably influenced by their experience with a predatory society and the feeling that they have to raise their kid to become a similar predator able to thrive in today's world. "A decent child would be left behind in society," and thus parents place a great emphasis on results. They want their kid to get straight A's and don't care as much about ethical behavior since it doesn't necessarily lead to the coveted objective.

The further choice of school is also influenced by this basic framework of their expectations. Owing to the assumption that ruthlessness is more important than decency and diligence, parents often choose a school where they feel their kids have the best chance of getting good grades:

> I also think that today parents prefer choosing a school that won't push the kids to a higher performance and a higher level of knowledge, but where the kids will breeze through everything.
>
> (Mrs. Hloušková, current vice-principal at Chestnut School; qualified to teach geography; ca. 59 years old).

Homework is an example of how this situation actually looks in schools. The school is expected to teach the kid everything, but preparing at home also contributes to good results. This preparation includes homework. Yet in the teacher's experience, no child does homework voluntarily. The teachers feel that the school should teach discipline, and one of the ways to do so is for the kids to do homework. Yet parents are often lax in their approach to discipline since they feel that a predator does not need it. A discussion on homework was held at Linden as part of the attempt at open communication with parents. This meeting was indicative of a vague search by the school for what was expected of it.

> You know, when I was hired in 1993, I was surprised that parents received a questionnaire on whether their kids would do their homework. There were three possibilities. The first choice was that they weren't going to do their homework at all; the second was that they'd do homework, but only if they wanted to; and the third was that they would do homework no matter what. And we marked in the class book A, B or C depending on the choice the parents made. And then we'd match it up with the kid so that we'd give this one a grade, but this one we didn't have to. So almost all the parents opted for the choice that they wouldn't do it at all, or the second choice. Later of course it became apparent that those kids wouldn't even go over the material at home. They wouldn't do it, not even look at it. Fortunately, this system was abandoned and everything was put back in order so that everyone had to do the homework. And now we're in the phase that we're trying to figure out what to do if the homework is not done. Since we don't have any recourse. So I write: he doesn't have his homework, for the third time, I write it in the class book. But that's all you can do. And another thing that happens a lot is

that the parents say that they don't want to be informed if their kid doesn't do his or her homework.

(Mrs. Okázalová, Linden School; qualified to teach history; ca. 42 years of age)

Behind these experiences is the uncertainty of who bears the actual responsibility for what the child learns and what kind of person he or she will be. Who should take the lead in this – the school or the family? Some teachers have their own theories on how the "responsibility vacuum" was created.

Because during communism the parents didn't bear responsibility; it was on the shoulders of the state. Although parents raised their kids, they essentially weren't responsible for them. I think that parents now have problems with taking on that responsibility. They aren't prepared to have responsibility, and yet they have a lot more of it. I think that sometimes they have problems coping with it.

(Mrs. Hanzelová, Linden School; qualified to teach Japanese studies, has an international certificate in English, the minimal level for teaching; ca. 44 years of age).

Another subject touched on several times during the interviews in connection with responsibility is that of alternating care of the child by divorced parents. If a kid is raised in two different homes by both parents, nobody bears responsibility. If a child forgets something, they can always say that it was forgotten with the other parent. Obviously, the teachers aren't opposing alternating care, they're just giving it as an example of how parents are often unable to bear the degree of responsibility that this complex situation requires.

Teachers feel that society expects the school to teach their kids everything – from proper behavior to knowledge. Teachers essentially agree with the notion that to educate also means to raise, but to what degree does this also concern the most basic things, like greeting someone?

It thus seems that parents' jobs and their lifestyle is most influenced by what teachers perceive as their expectations of the school as institution. The lack of time suffered by the parents' generation does not mean that the children have fewer needs, but that these needs have to be satisfied by someone else – and that someone is the teacher. The question then arises of what kind of teacher is required for this. The teacher Mrs. Poláková poses this question:

What does being a teacher entail then? He or she should to a certain extent be an expert, so this rules out the kind that needs to study up to grasp the subject. Then we need a mature person, and morally strong. But how do we know when that person is mature enough? Are you ready yet? Are you ready to teach? And on top of it all, are you able to communicate everything effectively to the kids?

(Mrs. Poláková, Chestnut School, qualified to teach Russian, music, today teaches English, ca. 45 years old).

The demands are therefore high. A teacher should be an expert, a morally strong person, an example for kids that accompanies them into adulthood. Being a teacher is largely a mission and a task. For many teachers this vision was the main impetus for attending the teacher's college; sometimes, however, they experience a genuine feeling of social prestige that the profession should have in their view. Yet here lies a great contradiction. The teachers feel this the moment they are confronted with other professions and the theoretical applicability in them. Respondents speak of completely contrasting experiences.

The subject of applicability and rating of teachers by the outside world came up several times during the interviews, though teachers only mentioned two specific situations. For the sake of completeness, I'm including both of these extreme examples:

A teacher is usually a very honest and conscientious person. One entrepreneur once told me that I should let him know if a teacher was leaving the school, that he'd employ the person right away. The reason is that the conscientiousness that the teacher possesses can be applied everywhere and every employer is looking for it.

(Mr. Neuman, Chestnut School; qualified to teach physical education; ca. 58 years old)

And the other, completely different example of how the surrounding world perceives teachers:

Well, when I was taking my social politics exam in college, my professor strongly insisted that teachers were the second most appreciated profession. That they were second on the list. Then there was a teacher at the exam, and he asked her how teachers were viewed in society, and she told him that it was more like at the bottom of the list. He got so upset [she laughs]. [...] I wanted to leave education, since I'd already had my fill of having kids, teaching kids and always being in the company of kids. So I told myself that I needed a break from it all. I'd say that as soon as they saw that I'd written on my CV that I'd been a teacher my whole life, they crumpled up the CV and threw it in the garbage. Because practically nobody got in touch with me. And it wasn't as if I was applying to be upper management of something. Or I had a really bad experience and left crying. ... this is a pretty good one, listen to this [she laughs]. I applied for a job through someone I knew at a pharmaceutical company. There was an opening for a company representative. The lady in human resources said that they really didn't like hiring teachers since they had bad experiences with them. When I asked why, she said that teachers are used to conducting a monologue and didn't know how to hold a dialogue. So I told her that's just her opinion and she said that it wasn't just her opinion, but a fact. And, she said, the people in their company are actually used to working. She told me that teachers end the day at noon and then go home, but that the people in their company would sometimes have to stay until evening and that it was a hard job. I left and was really hurt. I was upset. I really think that teachers aren't held in very high regard.

(Mrs. Kučerová, Linden School; qualified to teach first-level students and andragogy, ca. 39 years old).

During the interviews, teachers mentioned a number of times the feeling of not being perceived as equal partners by the kids, parents or society. Some respondents even said that they felt a certain drop in social standing, in prestige when they went to teach. The role of teacher has in their view weakened, though the respondents still see themselves as the guardian of values. Yet the contrast between values that are avowed in the families of the kids and those that a school tries to instill is often schizophrenic, which is also apparent in the prestige of the teaching profession.

Former principal Mr. Zámečník admitted in the interview that the problem isn't the kids as such. He and the teachers have noticed that kids have changed, but not in any fundamental way. The problem is deeper and lies in the relationship of the public to the school as an institution and in our idea of what should actually be happening in schools, what they should be like to help develop the next generation.

The question of the teacher's role does not just remain hidden behind the school walls. The teachers perceive the faltering of their values outside the school building as well, where, paradoxically, the contrast between the ideal and reality is in some case dramatized. One respondent recalled that once she had admonished a student outside the school. The parents came to complain because she had no right to comment on the behavior of their kid outside the school.

The following example also attests to the feeling of low social status that does not mesh with society's expectations of teachers and schools.

> Teachers are actually looked upon as a profession where after twenty years they're still making 18,000 crowns a month, which is horrible, while an entrepreneur makes... Our math teacher met here a former student that she'd flunked twice. He was sitting in a car that cost two and a half million crowns and he laughed in her face. I think that's a perfect example. The teacher has no prestige. If you look at it, we've got our own work schedule, everyone envies our long vacations, and that we go home at noon. But there are very few of us who go home and have a life. A normal teacher will study every evening the new EU-sanctioned methods, with their multifunctional tables and all, so every day, every hour you're working to grasp these new approaches. I can't imagine just arriving and teaching from the hip!
>
> (Mrs. Krečmerová, Chestnut School; studied to be a Czech language and art teacher, today teaches English; 51 years old).

Being a teacher means living with the following antitheses: Much work x little money; they're supposed to educate and raise x but must not interfere with kids' behavior outside the school; behavior at school x behavior at home; teachers should act as behavioral models x but nobody sees them that way since they don't have social prestige.

People from the town of Remízek, who worked as teachers, shed a slightly different light on the role of teachers in society. Mrs. Kelerová and Mr. Zámečník agreed that nobody from outside the school can bring back prestige to the teachers, but that the teachers themselves must make themselves visible and assume a more active position regarding the performance of their profession. According to town representatives, this can take the form of, for instance, the principals taking advantage of town events to present school activities, communicating with the town hall and being more active. The town hall would welcome this as well. Yet town representatives feel the teachers' attitude is somewhat different: If you invite us, we will come. The town hall calls for active partners, but there are apparently none to be found among the teachers. The problem is clearly who should return the prestige to teaching and how this should be done.

> I don't even know if teachers feel as if they can regain social prestige by being a certain way. That they bring their goods to the market and don't just grum-

ble that they're poorly paid and that the kids are naughty. [...] I think that they're hurting themselves. They'll never achieve social status by complaining that they don't have it.

They have to do something so that their group of people have it. And in order for them to have it, they need to be obliging, they need to be able to communicate with the other side.

(Mrs. Kelerová, Chestnut School, qualified to teach pedagogy, currently the deputy mayor of Remízek, 56 years old).

One of the respondents mentioned in this context the image of an equilateral triangle, whose top corner belongs to the parents, the second to the kids and the third to the teachers. In order for education to work well the triangle needs to be equilateral. All sides need to work together for education to succeed. This respondent felt that teachers had made a great step forward, but that the parents and the kids hadn't changed that much. In other words, in order for education to truly change, not only do teachers have to change for the better, but parents and kids need to as well. The active participation of all sides is a necessary condition. In connection with this, one respondent gave as an example the elective courses introduced at Chestnut for kids in the seventh grade and up. The range of courses is considerable – from art to philosophy. For a course to be available, there needs to be a sufficient number of enrolled kids. Unfortunately even the more gifted students opt for courses that won't require any additional significant effort – courses like gym class or art. Kids aren't interested in the more demanding courses for fear of their difficulty, and the parents don't encourage their kids to attempt them. Thus the school takes the initiative, but the response is weak. The question then is how to make an equilateral triangle from one that is not.

Which way forward?

At the end of the interviews I asked the teachers what they would like to see happen in the future. What they would change in education if they had a magic wand.

It was surprising to hear that there weren't many specific things that teachers felt they were missing. They are more bothered by what matters related to culture and values. Teachers would appreciate greater heterogeneity in the collective. They would welcome more male teachers working in schools. This would, in their view, change the atmosphere, in which the female elements currently predominate. More money and new equipment obviously would be welcomed. Modern equipment would enable the teachers to make use of all the know-how they acquired in the form of digital teaching aids that are currently gathering dust and represent a waste of the teachers' time. It would also enable them to interactively work with children and help them search for information and break up the static form of teaching.

With a reduced number of kids in the classes the teachers would better react to new requirements introduced by the reformed curriculum, and the demands of parents. In the past, teachers were mainly expected to present a lecture and have the students write dictation, having thirty kids in a class wasn't a problem. But if teachers are supposed to oversee the development of social relations, undertake projects and support kids in developing their own approach to education, then thirty kids per teacher is simply unmanageable.

On top of it all, teachers feel that it would help if the Ministry of Education finally got its act together, though the teachers didn't feel that this would happen under the current minister (at the time of the research Josef Dobeš – author's note).

> *As I say, the fish stinks from the head. First, I would put the Ministry of Education in order and establish a clear concept for education, for regional education, so that teachers know and can be sure that things will be a certain way. If there were a clear vision and objective, then we would head towards that goal. But if they keep changing the goal on us, then we'll flounder in it and lose patience with it. So that's the first thing. Unfortunately, the situation is as it is. So we are at least trying at our school to create a short-term objective. [Question: What kind of objective?]*
>
> *I'll summarize it for you. It consists of the satisfaction of the students, the satisfaction of the parents and the satisfaction of the teachers. That's it in brief. The results of the Czech School Inspectorate are not absolutely binding for us. In our view, it is important for the children to be satisfied, as well as the parents and teachers. I even presented this to the school authority and I think he understood.*

(Mr. Řehák, the current principal of Linden school; qualified to teach geography and Russian; ca. 50 years of age)

Teachers and principals are both calling for greater stability on the side of the government. The uncertainty of what else is coming slows them in adapting to the current conditions that the teachers feel are in many respects unsuitable. Greater stability would contribute to the discussion of the purpose of education, of what is the necessary minimum and which methods should be used to reach this minimum. How much should the kids memorize and how much should they be able to look up? The teachers give specific examples – e.g. should the kids understand Czech grammar in great detail? How much of this should the kids find themselves and to what degree are they already overwhelmed with information without being able to work and develop it independently?

The teachers also seem to think that upending the entire system is a greater problem than the system itself. In the face of all the changes, the teachers often repeated a mantra of sorts: "a six-year-old has remained the same since the days of Comenius." If with their magic wands the teachers were able to have the system concede this, teachers would be better off.

The greatest wishes concern that which is difficult to grasp, that which ensures quality of life and relations and which falls into the realm of culture, values, trust and hope, thus into almost metaphysical categories that the teachers would like to somehow make material with their magic wands. The insecurity that accompanied the interviews about the teachers' wishes tell us, however, that these things are the hardest to attain, since it depends only on specific people. It is not within the power of the individual to change values. A whole society is needed for this – groups and communities who consider these values as their beacons that their boat is heading for.

Teachers also suffer from the state of society that provides them with little support for their efforts. They also feel bad for the kids caught up in the social transformation who have lost their childhood and parents. And finally – teachers feel that their relations were for a certain period greatly disturbed by the political and social changes. Since relations at both schools returned in time to a state that teachers deem satisfactory, the fact that these relations can very easily go askew was evident in their responses. The anchor that held them pulled loose and still seeks a strong hold. The uncertainty regarding shared values in society and in their schools troubles them and they don't see any way out. And yet they feel that it actually wouldn't take much:

> We just need some of that sincerity, some of that calm, to stay a certain course. It doesn't depend on whether we have this kind or that kind of program, we still need to teach the child to read, write and count. And it's up to the teacher how to do it. Whether to do it through a game or some other way. But it has to be crammed into the kid. And not so that I'll be sitting behind a desk

and tell the kid to write the work. That's not the way. That has to change, the movement, the rest, the child has to be heard too. So many times we'd even scream during the class. I don't know how to explain it, but the person has to like it. And he has to devote time to it.

(Mrs. Slavíčková, Linden School; qualified to teach history; ca. 70 years of age)

5. Discussion and conclusions

The main question of the final part of this research concerns what we can take away from the teachers' testimony – what we learn from them about how our society works and the changes it has gone through. This final image is limited by the selection of samples – the respondents were teachers from two medium-sized primary schools in a small town. The main reason for researching this environment was an attempt at a deeper probe into the transformations of Czech society. The schools here are a microcosm of society and their environment presents a sample that allow us to grasp and discuss in specific situations the nature of these changes.

The qualitative character of the research will enable me in the final chapter to formulate several theories on the transformations of our society that can later be tested by related research in the future.

Teachers against a backdrop of historical and social changes

The teachers in the examined schools spontaneously divide their professional and personal life into the period before 1989 and the period after it. The social and political frame against whose backdrop teachers do their job has clearly played a fundamental role. This is usually in the form of an imperative and requirement by which the teachers encounter a situation in which they must in some way make a decision. These imperatives often take the form of a certain appeal that force teachers to choose between loyalty to the regime, to society or to their own convictions. Though this may have occurred to a greater extent prior to 1989, situations from the post-revolution period also showed similar traits.

Before 1989, teachers experienced several instances in which they had to make clear-cut choices. This largely applies to the period following the occupation in 1968 in which teachers were forced to declare their loyalty to the hardline communist regime. Teachers recall the vetting process with disgust and admit to appeasing the regime, giving various reasons for doing so: their situation at home, their desire to remain in the profession and even fear of blackmail, to name a few. Today they seek justification that would bring them vindication of sorts for their acts back then. It is not easy for teachers to recall these situations.

The same applies for their entire professional life under communism. On the one hand, teachers are largely convinced that politics don't belong in schools. Many teachers tried to forget about it and relegate it to the background when teaching, though they weren't able to escape it altogether. The creation of bulletin boards to commemorate political anniversaries, the celebration of political holidays, the obligatory preparation of the ideological use of selected course material and other communist requirements formed a framework for the entire school year and their day-to-day work. Today teachers interpret their performance of these requirements as a tax they needed to pay to be able to teach. They are consoled by the fact that every ruling regime places requirements of a similar nature on teachers. An important research finding was the respondents' attempt to justify their actions. The teachers did not view themselves as subservient tools of the communist regime. During this time they waged difficult little battles to save their souls and consciences. It would help if today's society moved away from its black-and-white view of the teaching profession and activities from that period.

In their testimony, the aspect of the communist regime prior to 1989 was more implicitly expressed in the form of an unspoken threat that if teachers didn't act a certain way, they'd encounter problems. Some teachers at both schools recalled colleagues with enough courage to stand up to the regime's requirements and were consequently punished as examples for others. One teacher at Chestnut who dared to leave a union meeting was bullied; at Linden, teachers recall a colleague fired during the normalization period because he had signed the protest document *2000 Words*. This shared recollection of possible punishment worked as a sufficient weapon to silence other possible rebels. We can therefore deduct that exemplary punishment works in a totalitarian regime as a powerful weapon that causes fear and, in turn, obedience.

Totalitarianism was also implicitly present in one aspect of a teacher's life. Though sometimes a prohibition was not explicitly declared, teachers were expected to know. According to the respondents, for instance, there was no list of banned authors or theories, and nowhere was it written that religious topics could not be discussed. Teachers were simply expected to know this and act accordingly.

Teachers generally adapted to these requirements of the communist regime. Now when speaking about this adaptation, they try to find instances that would provide justification from today's perspective. They thus speak of smaller struggles that led to the preservation of their personal integrity, recollecting times when they rebelled against some inane demands. It's apparent from their responses that most are ashamed of some of their past acts and worry about being denounced. I even came across teachers who refused to be interviewed due to this additional burden of shame. During the phase of authorizing their comments, some expressed the slightly exaggerated fear that they would be sued for what they said. There lingers the fear that their actions will be viewed through a black-and-white lens.

We can surmise from the interviews that in one area the teachers truly tried to preserve their integrity: in writing assessments of their students. At both schools it was clear that teachers tried to protect the kids and did not mention anything about their family backgrounds that could work against the students in their assessments. At Linden, teachers spoke of two cases in which negative assessments were given on students, but it was obvious that this was a unique situation. For the most part, archive records confirm this testimony.

When in direct contact with the kids, teachers made more of an effort to save face and their dignity, while also protecting the kids. It's not clear from the research whether this consisted of basic opposition to the communist regime, but it is apparent from the responses that teachers struggled more over the contact with the kids. Bulletin boards and the commemoration of communist milestones were a necessary evil, but the assessments were a complex part of the teaching professions requiring a great deal of diplomacy in which they needed to walk on eggshells.

Some teachers said that they did not feel any kind of pressure – or they claim with much conviction that they themselves did not experience similar dilemmas, since they had simply decided not to lie to the kids or to themselves. Yet these teachers can be seen as extremely mature and charismatic individuals who were ahead of their colleagues in considering the moral aspect of contact in the school. The contact with the kids was for them more than anything a kind of moral mission geared toward accompanying the kids into adulthood.

Why did teachers endure all of this? The reason seems to be that they genuinely wanted to teach. Over half of the respondents said they had wanted to teach from the time they were little kids. In their cases it was a fulfillment of childhood dreams that, unfortunately, ended up being realized in conditions that spoiled this dream with the harsh reality of life under communism.

Yet we also have to draw attention to the fact that the education system is and was filled predominantly by women. This is due to the organization of the school year, the advantage of summer vacations and a partially flexible work day that enabled them to combine a professional career and taking care of their families.

The year 1989 proved to be crucial not only from the perspective of social changes. The fall of 1989 ushered politics into the lives of teachers like never before. At Chestnut, these events led to the destruction of relations, from which the path of the collective's recovery has been long and painful. The school underwent a political purge of the so-called old structures from within – the collective was divided into two camps during the revolution – those who wanted to introduce a change and those perceived as representatives of the old establishment. The radical change of the principal was then a culmination of these events. A dividing line was drawn between those who at that moment stood on the winning side of the political barricade and those who found themselves on the losing side. Among those on the losing side there prevailed the feeling of being wrong since they felt as if they were being publicly denounced not because of their human or professional qualities but due to their formal membership in the communist party. They also felt as if this denunciation was not coming from people who had opposed the regime prior to November 1989, but by those who had long conformed to communist rule and had then opportunistically seized the moment.

There is still on the side of the victors a certain uncertainty and bitterness, and the question lingers of how the revolution could have been done differently. They distinguish between the normality of everyday life and revolutionary turmoil. From the perspective of the everyday, a blanket condemnation based on one's political affiliation seems less clear. In other words, the way in which changes were made could have been carried out less dramatically and destructively. But the turmoil of the revolutionary days was not conducive to clear thinking and perspective.

The Linden School maintained its relative apolitical character up until the competitions for posts; however, the destruction inevitably came, just a little later and for different reasons. All in all, the teachers from Linden feel that the situation before 1989 was relatively free of political burdens. The school maintained a professional level and in 1989 there really was no reason not to express confidence in the then leadership. Only later did the obligatory competitions lead the school to a new principal, and it was this change that marked the threshold of the destruction of relations. A different teaching approach was the common denominator of this change. Instead of order and discipline, a freer hand took charge that, as if in the name of the new political regime, denied the relevancy of former teaching methods and experience. The revolution seemed to have ushered in the rule that everything old is bad and anything new is better than the old, which is also apparent from published writings on the subject (Buraway – Verdery, 1999).

One paradox of the situation in Remízek is that many teachers, regardless of their political affiliation, left Linden to teach at Chestnut. This school also provided asylum to the former 'communist' leadership of Linden. The shake-up of 1989 brought about a situation in which it was decided (once again implicitly) that human qualities and professional competence were ultimately prioritized over political affiliation. It isn't exactly clear how this change occurred. One unanswered question is whether there was open consideration or more of a silent acceptance of the values that more correspond to the normalcy after the weathered storm. The recorded testimonies of teachers more support this latter version.

The year 1989 brought for many teachers a destruction of relations at both schools and a great hope for change in society, with which everyone in the late 1980s had long been dissatisfied. This hope was paradoxically shared by both communists and non-communists, by those involved in the revolutionary events and those who kept to the sidelines. The end of the dictate of the formalistic political establishment brought hope for new impulses and a new wind in the sails.

Teachers perceive the period after 1989 in several phases. They see the time immediately after the revolution until 1994/1995 as a phase of freedom that they enjoyed and that also did not place any dramatic demands on the way they taught. Some courses changed – obligatory Russian was replaced by English, and the kids no longer had to pass a defense training course in the old form. Yet fundamental changes were not made in the curricula; often they just replaced the word "socialist" with "democratic" in the teaching material and continued on. It brought to the entire system a little chaos in producing new books. Teachers had to choose the right textbooks; a centralized selection no longer provided any support and not all teachers were satisfied with the quality of new materials. In general, however, the turbulent political situation settled down and even in terms of relations, the teachers gradually entered calmer waters.

Following this post-revolutionary period a certain stagnation set in. Teachers don't recall any major events in education between 1995 and 2005. Everything settled into the new reality and no great changes occurred.

In this regard the reform begun in 2004 represents a strong impulse. Yet it wasn't the only source of changes; these are linked to other things as well. Linden came under new management in 2000, which immediately began to change the school and slowly tried to integrate new teaching methods and a new order within the possibilities of the given centralized curricula. The official school reform led more to an increase in administrative work at Linden. From a pedagogical standpoint, they had long ago experienced the reform – the Ministry of Education had, to the great aversion of school personnel, forced them to lay the administrative groundwork for it.

At this time at Chestnut, reinforcements arrived in the form of teachers of the younger generation, who brought with them new impulses to the school. Tensions between the generation began to appear with their arrival. The research was unable to fully uncover the essence and nature of this tension. Teachers from both generations described the troubles of today's school similarly, even using the same words. Nevertheless, both sides continue to feel that the different generations have a different take on the subject.

The reform and government requirements on teachers have produced new dilemmas that teachers feel resemble the pressures faced during the communist years. They once again find themselves in a situation in which the government is demanding something that they don't agree with, and they have to somehow deal with this personal disagreement.

Teachers agree that schools need a reform, but that the lack of concept and total decentralization is more to the detriment of basic education. Accompanying this are practical problems associated with e.g. students moving – due to the high degree of decentralization, a change of residence results in a truly stressful situation for teachers and kids.

Teachers' dilemmas before and after 1989

Most teachers have dilemmas linked to doing their jobs. There were more prior to 1989, but they occur today as well, even if to a limited extent.

In my view, dilemmas are a key indicator of a culture's transformation. We should also consider the meanings of the expressions "values" and "dilemmas", and how they are used in this study. Teachers often used the term "value" during the research. They feel it is a key term that expresses the shift in how their schools and the social world work. They usually use it to refer to a certain set of values that is strongly positive. This positive set of values is confronted with new – negative – values characterized by individualism and an emphasis on profit and effect.

However, in this research I intentionally did not ask teachers about values. In my view, the key indicator consisted of dilemmas. Dilemmas have the advantage that in specific situations they indicate the options that the respondents could choose from and how they legitimize their choices today. Specific complex situations call for the individual to decide between several ways of dealing with problems. Obviously everyone tries to make the correct decision, and so these situations are crucial from the cultural perspective. Ultimately, he or she must prioritize something. These dilemmas occur even in the most banal situations. What will I do when the principal tells me that family X goes to church, and that I, as the class teacher, neglected to include this piece of information in my assessment? What will I do when the district committee decides that the best student in my class won't be allowed to continue his studies because his or her family is frowned upon by the communist party? Dealing with these situations are a litmus test for the issues that are topical in a society.

Another key question that arose from the research is whether teachers had to do or say something that they didn't agree with or that they did not support. I have to admit that the question formulated in this way was not originally intended for the research. I originally attempted in the interviews to bring up the dilemmas in a different way. This mainly consisted of a direct question early in the research. But the teachers would always sidestep the question. They often evaded speaking in depth about the situation prior to 1989 by saying that the times were simply different and leave it at that. It was only after I reformulated the question that I managed to break through. Teachers actually pondered the question, often needing some time to respond. They themselves found the question to be interesting. And it was only in responding that they would gradually recall specific examples.

Their responses clearly need to be perceived within a present-day context. Teachers know how the story of doing their job turned out during the communist years. They also feel belittled for having worked as teachers during the pre-1989 period. On the other hand, I felt during the interviews that in recollecting specific events they had the urge to explain what it was like, what they had gone through in those situations and also to show that it hadn't been easy for them. They felt an aversion toward writing assessments, listening to political speeches at meetings and undergoing political training, etc., often perceiving it as a certain degradation and deeply considered their actions. Yet neither then, nor now, can they aptly express this feeling they had. I think that there are several reasons behind this "inability to express".

First of all, nobody has asked them about the period before 1989. Apparently, these interviews were the first time anybody had asked them about their experience prior to 1989.

Secondly, most of the teachers now feel ashamed for how they dealt with situations prior to 1989. They would have preferred to somehow convey the idea that they hadn't done everything automatically, out of their conviction, but due to the pressure they felt, out of a certain inevitability indicating the 'survival' mode in which they lived. Perhaps teachers still haven't found a way to aptly grasp and communicate this aspect of their careers.

There is also a third explanation. Teachers have already found the way to talk about their past. Their lament and distrust for the system, their enduring feeling that they are victims of the situation that took a turn for the worse after 1989 can simply be the attempt to say that the world is not that much better than it was, that there aren't that fewer dilemmas than before. And that therefore nothing really relevant happened. Their dilemmas during the communist years can in time seem slightly more bearable.

In my view, the questions on major dilemmas is crucial for understanding what is happening not only in education, but in society as a whole. Indeed, dilemmas are not only a thing of the past. Today's teachers must also deal with those that now arise. Their decision-making is, of course, qualitatively quite different, and yet these instances are important since deliberating over them shows us what is important for us and what we've already given up on, what we long for and what we consider to be forbidden. Dilemmas are the string connecting a dream with its possibility of being realized. But they can also signal a certain resignation that a dream can even be realized. What kind of dilemmas did our teachers then go through?

Prior to 1989 most teachers were confronted by a situation in which they knew and realized that the system represented by the principals and school inspectorate expected things from them with which they did not identify. Most decided to meet these requirements, usually in order to avoid major complications in their lives. Only a few teachers responded in the sense that they had not experienced any dilemmas. Their reason was generally a personal decision to maintain a certain authenticity.

Yet the teachers differ in the types of dilemmas they encountered. For some the bulletin board with propaganda was a necessary evil that hadn't warranted a second thought, and did not cause any dilemmas. For others the mere participation in any part of the communist structure, e.g. in a commission, was in itself a complex situation.

The situations in which teachers experienced dilemmas can be imagined as concentric circles. The further from the center, the smaller the dilemma. We can gather from the teachers' responses that far from the center would include speeches at the school in commemorating communist anniversaries, creating politically oriented bulletin boards, paper collection for recycling, etc. Somewhat closer to the circle's center are then political meetings and training, being nominated to various commissions and posts in the school or in society. Still closer to the center consisted of writing assessments, preparing class work on political subjects, etc. An inspection or any other external check of the school occupies the second closest position to the center. The very center is represented by the offer to become a communist member. The closer to the center, the less it concerns banal experiences and the more it touches on the soul and integrity.

This scheme does not only apply for the small group of respondents that fully identified with the regime prior to 1989. They feel that there was nothing wrong with the regime's requirements. Over the course of the research I found only three such respondents, two of whom held management positions in the school during the normalization period.

The principals of both school were in a slightly different situation. They had themselves helped to create the regime. Yet this is only partly apparent from their answers. They more saw themselves as subordinates than as those who had the power to somehow influence the course of things and events. The two principals also differ in reflecting on their work in that position.

The former director of Chestnut School prior to 1989 still defends the ideals of communism of the 1950s as she was strongly influenced by her leftist family. She sees herself as someone who became principal merely as a result of the way things unfolded. Today she mostly recalls her years as principal in terms of the great responsibility for the building and property and her great personal and work commitment. All in all she doesn't feel that she could have somehow had a fundamental impact on things.

The principal at Linden represents a more pragmatic approach oriented towards perfect professional performance. As an acknowledged expert in chemistry and the principal of the school, she wanted above all for everything to run perfectly at the school. Due to her involvement in the communist party, she was, according to her subordinates, able to use this perfect functioning to create a protective wall of sorts between the school and the communist governing bodies so that politics would not burden the teachers in their work. Apparently this worked, for there were a fewer number of dilemmas prior to 1989 in the responses of teachers. This almost idyllic picture is disrupted only by the unwillingness of one respondent to be interviewed because she is still ashamed of how she behaved before 1989 and how she blindly followed orders. One question is to what extent today's recollections of the past are conditioned by an awareness of the political changes and by the polarity reversal of the value orientation in society.

Teachers' assessment of the dilemmas also depends on how they acted in 1989. The year 1989 is seen as extraordinary. One cannot prepare for a revolution, and reacts differently at the given moment than under normal circumstances. The responses clearly showed a difference between normal life and the unrest of the revolution. The respondents feel that a revolution provides the opportunity for non-standard reactions. The assessment of these acts still isn't clear after twenty years. One uncertainty concerns the personal profile of the individuals involved. It's certainly not as clear from today's perspective that membership in the party would necessarily require the individual to step down from a leadership position or that those who had been loyal to the regime just a few days before the events of 1989 began had the right to organize the revolution. Who determines who was good and who was bad, "who is the hero and who is the traitor"? These questions still linger with relevancy.

Teachers still aren't sure whether they acted properly at the time. A certain calming of relations several years after the revolution indicated that the attempt to maintain relations was more important than political affiliation at that time. Another explanation stem from the fact that Remízek is a small town and the attempt and willingness to preserve good relations can be given by the fact that people don't want to leave the town, to sell their home and move. At any rate, the clashes and personal antipathies were not so strong after the revolution to force those involved to move away from Remízek.

The dilemmas following 1989 are more of a minor nature and are linked more to the relationship to the government. The teachers do not believe in the system and its requirements. Their willingness to participate in changes dictated from above is thus minimized to carrying out administrative requirements linked to the reform. Teachers do not have *a priori* convictions against reform, but they feel that it will once again lead to an increase in administrative pressure and not to a real qualitative change. However, reference to present-day dilemmas in their responses may also conceal an unwillingness to invest time and energy to actual qualitative changes in their schools. The constant personnel changes at the Ministry of Education merely provides an excuse to dismiss any current government vision since it will all come to naught with the next elections. It is then easier to consider the impulses of each new minister as a mere cosmetic matter that most likely won't have any bearing on the teachers' everyday effort in the classroom. This feeling of necessary evil in connection with the reform was evident at both schools. Yet there was also the attempt at both schools to derive something positive out of the school reform. If, however, the teachers were able to make a positive change, the feeling prevails that it was done in spite of the system and not with its help.

The new qualification requirements for the individual teachers was another major topic at Linden. The fact that teachers with vast experience and the wrong diploma had to leave the school is further proof that formalism wins out over common sense. Though teachers understand the government's attempt to improve the quality of education, they comment dryly that forcing out superb and experienced teachers a few years before their retirement merely because they have the wrong diploma will not bring about this positive change.

The transformation of the school culture

The school's culture represents an intricate web of relationships, symbols and rituals, and shared stories from the present and past. The basic transformation of society that the revolutionary wave brought to both schools, also caused the school culture to change. The question is which aspects of the school culture have changed and which haven't.

The entire communist world of symbols and rituals collapsed in 1989. The symbols and rituals that were strictly bound to the political regime prior to 1989, dissolved practically overnight. The question quickly arose of who would introduce new rituals and what kind of form they would take.

This subject is nicely represented by the situation at Linden, where a new principal was hired after 1990. He immediately set about having a sacred place related to the Second World War removed from the school's foyer. Principal Zámečník considered this move necessary, since he hadn't wanted the youngest students welcomed into the school by depressing images from concentration camps. At the same time he felt directed at him the outrage of the teachers, who considered this step as disrespectful toward established customs. This is just a minor example of the disappearance of old symbols, but also of their removal being perceived as a clear declaration of dissent with the pre-revolution period.

New traditions gradually emerged at both schools – for instance, the Christmas mixer, or events for local preschools and homes for the elderly. But not everything started up immediately and it took some time for the new customs to take root.

Relations at both schools were put to the test during the revolution, though it does seem that following those tumultuous times they did return to the standard that teachers were used to before 1989. The research thus confirms some theoretical premises that relations have greater persistence and do not change as quickly as political systems (Marková, 2004).

The teachers at Linden spoke of enduring smooth relations. These Linden teachers would organize and carry out together a wide range of activities; they were a group who spent free time together, went on trips and to the pub together. Many teachers left the school after 1990 and it took a while for the new teachers to get to know and become friends with the others. Yet today teachers feel that relations are back on a good level, that the school's atmosphere is once again friendly and that teachers once again want to spend free time together.

More than politics itself, it was the social situation of the various families of the teachers that brought about a change in relations. Previously everyone had received similar wages and was roughly as well off as the next person. This applied to their spouses as well. All teachers were more or less on the same social level. Then, after 1989, some would become more enterprising, some would stay on the same level, and some would find themselves worse off. Social stratification resulted in complications of e.g. deciding which restaurant to go to, what teachers could afford to buy or where they could spend their holidays. Teachers mentioned social differences as an aspect that divides people.

The post-revolutionary period also brought with it increased pressure on work performance, which logically means less time for maintaining friendships. The faster world requires that teachers return right home after school. Respondents gave insufficient time as the reason why they didn't spend as much time together.

The above also applies for Chestnut School, where the initial situation concerning relations also eventually returned to the pre-revolutionary state. But this differed from Linden. There prevailed at Chestnut prior to 1989 greater tension among teachers than at Linden. Although teachers recall a pleasant and easy-going atmosphere in the staff room, the faculty was visibly divided into groups. The same is apparent at the school today. Respondents mentioned clear indications of conflicts between generations at Chestnut both prior to 1989 and after.

Yet that which applies to relations among teachers does not hold true for parents and kids. Here we see a much greater shift. It is apparent from the research that relations between parents and teachers underwent a markedly positive change. Parents feel that the school has significantly improved compared to the pre-1989 period. They feel that teachers consider them partners, that the kids matter greatly to the teachers and that the teachers attempt to see the good in them and develop their potential. This positive change mainly consists of the trust that the teachers want to do well by them and their kids. Yet the system itself did not deserve the parent's trust, just the individual teachers.

This finding is interesting in light of the concept on slow changes in relations (Marková, 2004). It's clear that trust in relations can work as a certain catalyst. Trust is the first step toward improved relations. The question is whether changed relations based on trust have in the future the potential to transform the entire system and its structures.

Although teachers try to understand parents in their situation, they are for the teachers a source of new uncertainties and dilemmas. In the teachers' view, parents have clearly acquired a greater realm to influence what goes on in the school. Sometimes this power is positive, but it can also possess a threatening nature, as when, for instance, some teachers are forced to leave a school after parents intervene. Teachers from both schools referred to such instances, though it seems that they were more often linked to Chestnut.

In the teachers' eyes, the parents embodied the changed **value system** that greatly troubles teachers at present. Due to their increased work load, parents don't have time for their kids, and this has many consequences. Teachers have the feeling that children do not receive from home as solid a value base as before. This is partly because parents don't have time and partly because the teachers feel that society no longer agrees on which values are actually positive.

According to the teachers, this kind of social agreement could help alleviate their feeling that parents are caught in a crossfire of values. Assuming the position of an "authority on values" would facilitate discussions on what is right and wrong in schools. But since there is no reservoir of values, performance and efficiency win out, and this suppresses values linked to a sense for the collective, an ability to listen and a willingness to yield and help those weaker. Yet all this merely inhibits a rapid and efficient ascension on the social ladder, and teachers aren't sure whether they should try to teach kids these skills and habits. Every family raises kids differently, and these values and views converge and sometimes even collide at schools.

When faced with this implicit clash, teachers are more likely to remain conservative proponents of what they consider to be old values. They feel that discipline, respect, the ability to take a step back and help are very important in the education of kids. Unfortunately, they feel alone in their convictions and aren't sure whether they share this value system with parents – not to mention society at large.

This clash of values becomes all the more apparent in the collective of kids. A survey clearly showed that kids feel less safe in a collective with other kids their age and trust each other less, even less than they trust their teachers.

This is sensed by both parents and teachers. According to all involved, kids behave much worse than before, social differences play an increasingly larger role beginning in the first year of school, and kids often do not show respect to parents or teachers.

This conclusion is largely influenced by the fact that each generation has a more or less critical view of kids, which teachers admit to with a sense of humor. On the other hand, parents and teachers agree that kids have changed too much. It's as if kids have paid the price for the radical transformation, that the pressure for greater performance has worked to suppress traditional values oriented on the family and society.

Another uncertainty that has emerged with regard to teaching kids concerns the means that are currently appropriate. Teachers have ceased to use corporeal punishment, but neither teachers nor parents are completely sure whether it wouldn't be a more effective means than the endless poor conduct marks they give and which don't seem to have any effect. Teachers feel that no matter what method they use they have little chance of imposing their will, so they lessen their requirements on the kids and sometimes even give up on how they feel a class should be taught. For instance, they don't check whether students do their homework or they lower their standards of students' knowledge in the exact sciences.

The same applies for parents. Parents tersely described this trend at parent-teacher meetings at Linden, saying that they don't apply greater pressure on their kids for fear that they will attempt to leave home for good. This wasn't just the solitary voice of a single parent; it was evident that most parents present held the same concern.

It would be worth further studying parents' attitudes since they aptly capture the uncertainties of our age. The unsure way in which they raise their kids could in the future serve as a map for a discussion on shared values in society and could help them in their search.

The school culture also includes the creation of a certain **continuity** and the sharing of stories. Whether those involved share their stories, whether they tell positive or negative stories, who tells them and how the tradition and history is present at a school is another indicator of school culture and its quality. Several important trends have appeared in the realm of sharing stories and preserving continuity.

At both schools it is as if a living history began in 1989. Nevertheless, the two schools formally declare on their website a history dating back to their founding. Linden even recently celebrated 100 years of its existence, commemorating the event with photo documentation on its website. Yet it is different with the living history. Teachers who worked in the schools prior to 1989 said that I had been the first to ask about their pre-1989 experiences. Not one of the former teachers mentioned that they had, for instance, been invited to the school to take part in a discussion; they feel that nobody is interested in the school's history. Events of the past forty plus years are not reflected upon and not an integrated part of the lives of the two schools. This feeling of discontinuity became all the more apparent when I was unable to find out whether the school has a chronicle from that time at its disposal, and by the fact that the town's chronicle held extremely brief records of the time, assessments had been shredded, etc. It is as if the revolution took away the continuity and that it still hasn't been recovered.

This dividing line is relatively understandable in political matter. The interpretation of late communism, the events of 1989 and the period following it is very complex for all of society. Yet the discontinuity in shared stories in other areas is dumbfounding. For instance, at Chestnut none of the respondents mentioned the school's great successes in sports. The contradiction between the teachers' critical view of their school and the overview of recent successes in sports, recorded in the local chronicle, was shocking. How can this be? Why aren't these successes a catalyst in the life of a school that everyone can be proud of?

This contradiction can be interpreted by using the concept of a toxic culture and also offers great potential for the school's further development. A new understanding of the past combined with the right stories of the present can bring the required impulse. Sharing the joy from a school's successes and reflecting upon the past twenty years could teach the kids not only respect, but also provide them with a deeper understanding of what the world of their parents went through.

The transformation of the concept of education

Teachers' responses to the parts of the research on dilemmas, school culture or educational reform points to some deeper roots of the state in which education currently finds itself. Indeed, much more has changed. Teachers speak of substantial changes in overall expectations by the school, but also perceive their different role and the change in the values of society a whole, which is clearly reflected in their work.

In examining the research findings, it was clear that teachers are searching for a certain type of causality that would enable them to describe the current situation in education. Yet in analyzing their responses in detail, we see that their logic used to explain the current situation turns into a wicked circle which seems to have no way out.

I will first try to sketch this circle, or better yet two circles joined to form a small infinity. In the conclusion, I'll try to indicate a way out of this enclosed system. Clearly, the lingering question is whether the system of a wicked circle that offers no prospects can be changed into a new system that would open and offer possible paths. Let us first take a look at the individual parts of this wicked circle as described by the teachers:

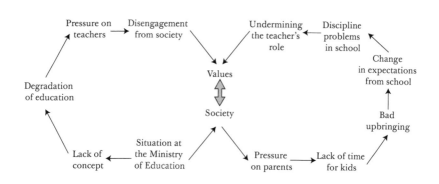

Social changes and the transformation of the value system related to them are, in the eyes of the respondents, central for understanding the current situation. In their view, the post-1989 world consists of a squandered chance. They feel that the people who came into power in society opened the value system to a dog-eat-dog world with profit as the measure of success in life. Yet teachers hope for something other from the new post-1989 system than the 'social centrifuge' that they found themselves in.

The teachers characterize the situation after 1989 as an unstable period that blindly reversed values, which led to today's unanchored state. The new period automatically deemed everything from the past as bad and vice versa without reflecting more deeply upon what society actually wanted and which direction it should take.

If superficial impressions sufficed, it might seem that in their recollections teachers prefer the period before 1989 as a period in which the value system, and thus orientation in society and in relations was easier and brought a greater quality of life. It might seem as if a certain nostalgia emanated from their responses. However, such a perception would be in direct contrast with the dilemmas that teachers went through in the pre-1989 period.

In further examining the responses, another interpretation is offered that brings a new dimension to the overall picture of the changed value system. In their responses, the teachers distinguish between two value systems: The one before 1989 and after it provided them with basic orientation in relation to the system. The other provided orientation in everyday contact between people. While the first system is more held in their memories as a willingness to adapt and, if possible, not hurt anyone, the second is represented by the image of proper behavior and upbringing, thoughtfulness and a sense for good relations. After 1989 the following occurred: The value system geared toward everyday contact between people radically changed. Teachers feel that impoliteness, an emphasis on individualism and the pressure for performance and profit now prevail. Yet the values related to the system have not changed. The teachers once again go by the motto "having your cake and eating it too."

They negatively rate the current state since, from today's perspective, they used to at least internally identify with how people acted towards each other. They feel that today's world has lost its basic social customs regarding interpersonal relations and has become much more coarse. There are exceptions to this rule – good relations in the staffroom and relations with some parents serve as examples that some things can thrive. But these are still merely exceptions to the overall feeling of a social jungle.

Thus life in a dual truth (Marková, 2004) that was typical for the period before 1989 largely endures today and is fundamentally linked to the matter of trust in society. A lack of trust prevents the integration of two value systems; each separately applies to one of the worlds in a disjointed reality.

This question of values can be interpreted in a slightly different light. It's clear that both teachers and parents have unsure footing in specific dilemmas – situations in which they must make decisions. And they are also seeking a clearer orientation. Prior to 1989 this orientation was largely determined by the rules bound to the education system. The nature of the dilemmas was more of an internal struggle about which nuances it was still possible to adapt in, and in which it was no longer possible.

After 1989 the nature of the dilemmas changed – all decisions can be easily made and have real effects. The problem is that there lacks authority that would endorse such decisions. Thus the mantra of a value system also becomes a call for this authority. The world full of uncertainties would be much simpler if there was at least a fixed frame of values. This is precisely what teachers feel is missing. It can explain why during the interviews teachers often spoke of a value system even without being specifically asked about it. The specific dilemma-situation led respondents to more general thoughts on searching for a common system that to a certain extent would offer a guaranteed response in these specific dilemma-situations.

Teachers aren't only upset about the new world's coarseness in theory; they speak about it because they encounter its consequences eight hours a day when teaching.

This fast-paced world, propelled by a desire for profit and visible success, creates a new situation for entire families. **Parents** are under great pressure to meet these requirements. As a consequence of this effort not to lose work or simply to meet the demands of the new world, they spend most of their time at work and don't have any time for their **kids**. When speaking with parents it's obvious that they would like things to be different. They would like to spend a lot more time with their kids. Unfortunately, they don't know how to mesh their work and family obligations. They try not to waste the little free time left for their children on conflicts over how to raise them. So the kids end up living without being raised in a set way.

Obviously, this varies from family to family, as does the degree to which they feel work pressures. Presently, however, families are faced with a number of complex situations for which there are no instructions. There has been an increase in the number of divorced families and families where the mother has left. The foundation is unstable and attempts at raising kids in this wobbly world lose their clear direction.

Teachers feel that the **parents' expectations of the school** have changed due to increased pressure on performance. The basic antagonism in the expectations is the relation between upbringing and education. What should the school actually do? Teachers at both schools agree that more is now expected from schools than before. Teachers feel that society wants the school to do everything, to educate and raise their kids. The reason is that families have too much pressure at work and don't manage to raise their kids themselves, so they look for an ally. The school seems to be the logical choice of institution to take over some of these duties. This perception corresponds with the increasing pressure for children to remain as long as possible in after-school care. In fact, during this research the hours of before- and after-school care were extended upon the parents' request.

Teachers and parents thus essentially agree on the demands imposed on the school. But in reflecting upon this state, teachers feel that they are at the end of their tethers. In their view it's understandable that the kids should learn to function in a broader society at school and that school attendance is one of the behavioral aspects of this. On the other hand, the kids need to have learned certain fundaments of behavior at home. It is becoming increasingly evident to teachers that some kids are not getting any of these fundaments from the family, and it is hard for them to catch up just by attending the required classes.

Disciplinary problems are then according to teachers and parents merely a logical consequence of the above. Kids are less a collective in class, they are more reluctant to integrate those who are different, and kids behave to each other and to teachers with unprecedented insolence (e.g. playing poker during class, giving excrement as a Christmas gift, drugs in schools). Adults have deprived the kids of their childhood and not replaced it with anything new and positive. So equipped with the deafening loud music playing out of their headphones, kids don't learn to talk and listen to others.

Teachers have noticed many differences between kids from cities and smaller towns. The smaller the community and less complex the social network, the more kids have remained kids. At least that's how the situation is assessed by teachers who have taught in different settings and can more aptly make the comparison.

In the view of the lost childhood, teachers and parents differ in one aspect. While teachers feel that kids spend too much time at school and are overburdened and have less space for everyday games and playing around, parents don't feel that their children have too much work. Instead they have the impression that their kids could spend even more time at school. This aspect would need complementary research on the structure of kids' time at basic schools and on the way they spend their time with their families, friends and other types of entertainment.

Teachers interpret the coarseness of the children's world as a plea for contact. They would like to better mediate to the children this personal dimension of coexistence in the school, but they are unsure of how to do it in classrooms with headcounts that rule out any chance for a more personal approach.

From this perspective, teachers feel that the demands on their previously defined role is changing, and are unsure of what exactly their position entails. It's clear that they cannot satisfy all these demands at once.

We can also see that the **role of teachers** in society is fluctuating and its definition is also changing. Prior to 1989 the teachers were, whether they liked it or not, largely an extension of the communist regime, while after 1989 they were forced to become buffers of a certain type of change – some subjects were done away with and there arose new qualifications and great changes in society that gradually made their way into education. All this forms the context in which teachers work. They themselves then had to define this new role.

On the one hand, teachers today feel as if they are quixotic defenders of traditional values. Yet they feel as if an emphasis on discipline, respect and social sensitivity is a set of values that most of society does not share with them. One of the pessimistic results of the research is that to a certain extent teachers feel removed from society for whom they are raising the next generation. Teachers feel that society is presently controlled by a desire for profit and an aggressive life style, with which they don't agree and don't share. Their daily struggle in classes is also one to preserve the remaining values of the world they were used to and believed in. These values are not dependent on politics but on the support of a collective spirit, a sensitivity towards other and the perception of the surrounding world not only as a space for fulfilling one's own immediate desires.

Since teachers feel that the current trend in society is to view others in terms of their salaries, the low wages in education aren't much of a help in this. Teachers feel that though the demands on their job performance have increased, their social status has diminished due to their low salaries. This makes it all the more difficult for them to hold the position of moral authority when the rest of the world doesn't see them that way.

This leads us from the first part of the wicked circle, which describes the situation in the field, to how teachers perceive society's levels above them.

Teachers do not feel that the **Czech Ministry of Education** is a trust-worthy institution due in part to the rapid turnover of the various ministers, and to the murkiness of their overall concept. Teachers don't find anything on the government level that would convince them that it has any vision and willingness to truly support schools. When teachers speak of the government, they often mention a few of the visible consequences of its recent activities.

1) **The creation of school educational programs**: Teachers had to draft the curricula for their school in their own free time and without remuneration. Although teachers approached this task in a different way at the two researched schools, both attempted to use this assignment to make improvements. In general, however, teachers do not agree with the complete decentralization of curricula. But the mere thought of having to get rid of the current system and create a new one is even more terrifying for them. They therefore feel that at the moment it's better to stay with the concept that is now in place than to go back to the old way a few years down the line. Teachers would then recommend attempting to improve the current concept instead of making another complete overhaul.

2) **Pressure on using new teaching methods**: Teachers feel that the outside world is calling for the maximum application of new teaching methods. The teachers perceive a certain antagonism between cramming and a freer approach to teaching. During the interviews the teachers openly reflected upon what actually is needed more and how demands for both can currently be met. They agree that kids need both, that they need to learn a strong foundation of facts. Teachers feel that this way of learning is important for building one's memory and for later skills

combining knowledge from different disciplines. Yet teachers are also aware that there is a need to teach children how to work with the information. However, a necessary condition for both is a certain discipline and respect in schools, which brings us back to the questions of relations and culture. Teachers are lacking in these efforts a clear task. Where do they stop cramming kids full of information and begin with skills working with this information. Is the current standard properly set and does it really meet today's demands? These are merely further questions arising from the research and that would warrant their own study.

3) **Degradation of education**: Teachers are troubled by the departure of students from schools following the fifth grade. On the one hand teachers understand this and, faced with a similar decision about their kids, would choose out of fear of the second level a more difficult grammar school. But as professionals they see the consequences of this decision. With the increased pressure for a formal education that teachers feel does not necessarily fit with currently applicable skills and knowledge, teachers believe that the distance has increased between the grade that the student receives and the actual level of knowledge it is supposed to represent. Kids who passed primary school only because teachers had mercy on them are graduating with high school diplomas. Much of the class leaves to attend grammar schools, so the primary school becomes a dumping ground for the less successful. Teachers don't want to push for the abolition of 6- or 8-year grammar schools, but they wonder about the consequences of a premature division of kids into the more or less successful. The eight-year gymnasium should not be the normal educational trajectory, but a place for truly exceptionally gifted kids. Such gymnasiums cannot, however, be banned, but the entire system needs to be gradually and systematically changed.

Teachers and parents do not agree on whether today's education is more difficult than it used to be when parents went to school. Teachers believe that they can no longer use their old teaching material for the exact sciences since grammar schools are not able to work out the examples from the basic school. Parents, on the other hand, feel that the material is too difficult and they can't keep up with it. This too begs the question of what actually kids should be learning in schools and to what detail.

Uncertainties surrounding the functionalities of the entire system not only increase the pressure on teachers, who find themselves in situations they are unable to cope with, but also intensify their feeling of detachment from a society that has differing values and does not provide them with conditions that would facilitate their work.

This closes the wicked circle of causalities and brings us back to pondering the social changes and their influence on the situation in today's schools.

Despite this wicked circle, most teachers taking part in the research are satisfied with their work. The most enjoyable part of their job is contact with the kids and the feeling that, despite everything, they are able to have a positive influence on them. At both schools the teachers have created a microcosm on which they hope the outer world's changes have the least possible effect, and are satisfied with this microcosm. The world of children is a challenge for them that they enjoy. Despite all the negative consequences for them, the regime change at least offered them possibilities to influence the world around them more than before.

Which way out of the vicious circle

In returning to the theoretical bases of this work, we have a chance to ponder the responses in still a different light.

It's clear that a transformation is a process that brings about a change in society owing to the desire to get from point A to point B (Sztompka, 2003). Yet we see that during this movement the schools experiencing that which occurred in other post-communist countries as well. The prevailing belief was that anything new was better than the old, communist way (Buraway – Verdery, 1999) and often the values were automatically reversed, though not always leading to a positive result. Discipline, cramming facts into students and other attributes of teaching before 1989 were automatically perceived negatively and replaced by other approaches that were often the opposite. But the blind application of these methods also resulted in difficulties. At present it's as if the pendulum has swung back and only now is the best golden middle path being gradually considered. It is, however, highly probable that this search for the golden middle path will take much time since it again requires changes in both the structure and culture (Fullan, 2000).

It's evident from the research that neither the changes in the structure, nor in the culture were completely successful in Czech education. The structural changes did not yield the necessary faith in the system. Teachers don't have faith in the changed structure and don't feel that it's something that helps them in teaching.

Of interest is one basic contradiction that systematically appears in the teachers' responses. On the one hand teachers complain that they don't receive from the Ministry of Education and other education bodies tasks that would help them with their jobs. On the other hand, they negatively perceive the school reform that brought with it boundless freedom. It's therefore evident that the teachers themselves are unsure and lack a clear vision of what they expect from the system. They want more freedom, but they feel that there's too much freedom in education. This paradox can perhaps only be explained with the help of Holmes (1997), Marková (2004) and Dahrendorf (2005), who speak of an unsettling of values. An uncertainty of roles and values dramatically increases expectations posed on leaders, authorities and structures, who, however, don't actually perform this role of savior and can't perform it in society. These above scholars feel that this automatic expectation of authorities is a typical post-communist attribute.

This uncertainty among teachers then obviously emerges in uncertainties in determining the true objectives of education. In this sense, the 2004 reform actually brought more questions than answers. Teachers expect a clear response to the question of what kids should learn at primary school and how they should teach it. Yet the completely decentralized system does not provide them with an answer to this.

Teachers are exasperated. Although the individual schools invested a great deal of work into preparing their school educational programs, they feel that it didn't bring any positive effect. Yet they also refuse to return to centralized curricula. They feel that such a backward step would only increase their overall frustration.

It's most likely that a certain type of document, clearly stating the rules under which the entire system would run, could clarify the educational objectives in this situation. According to the original reform plans, this document was to be the National Educational Program, based on paragraph 3 of the Educational Act from 2004. The document was to have been created from a broad public discussion, but the plan was never realized and thus the state did not carry it out in accordance with what the law stated. Instead of the National Educational Program, general educational programs were drafted straight away, which, however, without this overarching document only added to the uncertainty of the entire system.

The addition of a hierarchy of documents covering current education could help in elucidating the entire system. One question is how to restore credibility to the system. Teachers feel that such credibility has been lost and that schools perceive instructions from the government in more of a negative light. Neither teachers nor principals have the feeling that they are equal partners for the government, and this basic relationship of distrust is evident in their reluctance to accept suggestions from above.

A change of culture should therefore not only occur on the level of the individual schools, but also fundamentally on the central level. Indeed, trust and credibility are cultural attributes of a system that cannot be changed by decree or document. Trust needs to be built through conscientious communication, in which schools feel that there is a willingness to view teachers and principals as partners and professionals that are part of the dialogue.

A lingering question then is why teachers even need the government to make changes in specific situations at their schools. Why are they looking for the government to alleviate their frustration? Data from the research offers an explanation in the form of a certain unimaginativeness that brings us back to values. Teachers repeatedly face situations in which they try to do something, they have a certain idea how to resolve certain situations, but in carrying out this solution they run up against an illogical, formal obstacle that changes the original good intention into a farce. For instance, teachers are supposed to use new methods and cultivate good relations with the kids, but their colleagues, whom others see as experts and excellent teachers, are not allowed to remain at the school due to new laws concerning formal qualifications. Teachers seek a culprit in these situations since they repeatedly have someone somewhere thwarting their efforts. Quality thus comes into conflict with the witless utilitarianism of a system void of values.

Research on the change of culture on the level of central authorities would be worthwhile.

A change of structures, which is the government's main task, and a change of culture, without which there can be no vision for the changes of structures, should go hand in hand. It's as if the central level remains shrouded in the mist and it would be worth knowing what propels development on the central level forward. The processes of change could then be more transparent and they would provide better orientation in the field; there wouldn't just be instructions to fill out even more dull forms. Orientation from the state would provide clear signals on the future direction of education that advances (or slows) today's information-based society.

The biggest area for further work is thus the question of values – those already experienced at both schools, those that motivate changes on the level of the Ministry of Education, or those that propel the development of our society. The instability of values at present does not provide sufficient orientation for key roles in our lives – what it means to be a teacher, how a parent should be, what are the borders of respect, what it means to negotiate, etc. These are all questions that arose with the post-1989 world and for which we continue to seek answers.

We can imagine the transformation as a spring or a taut rope with culture on the one side and structure on the other. This middle ground is ideal since it represents a perfect balance that is not, however, static. It's a dynamic search for the middle ground where the pressures are balanced out. This is determined by the relations between the change of culture and the change of structure, whereas structures rapidly change, but can't work well without changes in culture. We saw this in both the theoretical part as well as in the teachers' various situations. And if we adopt a top-down and bottom-up approach to the tension between structure and culture, we have the entire system that delineates the space in order to map events at both of the monitored schools. Until now the situation seems to be that the current status forces teachers into the role of victims of circumstances; the question is whether this basic terrain also offers a way out of the vicious circle.

If we take seriously the postulate of the relationship of structure and culture, and we thoroughly examine the wicked circle of causalities that the teachers see, we notice one important thing. Each of the point of this circle possesses the potential for not only a change of structure, but also a change of culture. Take for example the relations of teacher and parents that are formed, among other places, at parent-teacher meetings. In visually presenting what takes place on the level of culture and structure in two monitored classes, we arrive at the following chart:

	Structure	Culture
Chestnut	During the parent-teacher meetings the kids aren't present at the school. Parents stand in an inhospitable hallway where there's no seating and wait in line to talk with the class teacher who is speaking with parents in the classroom.	Symbols: a line to see the teacher, empty class, no kids around; Rituals: The order in line determined by "first come, first serve"; Relations: none or minimum communication between parents; individual conversation with class teacher; Values: Respect for privacy, individualism.

	Structure	Culture
Linden	The kids spend the entire afternoon baking a cake with the teacher; the classroom is prepared, a large table is in the middle around which the parents gather. The kids serve them coffee or tea and then wait for their parents in the hall.	Symbols: refreshments, a gathering around the table; Rituals: leading parents to the classroom, preparing refreshments; Relations: a shared space, a community of parents, communication between the parents, less space for individual conversations with the class teacher; Values: A friendly space, a collective experience.

The impulse to introduce a different way of organizing parent-teacher meetings is given in both classes by a shift in values of the class teachers. At Chestnut the class teacher wanted to provide more space for a personal, less formal meeting with parents and prioritize consultation-like meetings. To a certain extent the teacher was trying to make a distinct change from past customs when parents sat at desks like the kids and she would speak to them all at once.

The Linden class teacher thought long and hard how to get parents more involved and to make the parent-teacher meeting pleasant.

We see then that a certain cultural mission intended to bring a positive change is behind the current form of parent-teacher meetings. Both class teachers moved on the axis between the cultural and structural. A cultural mission was the catalyst for changing the form of parent-teacher meetings; this led the teachers to change the structure (arranging the room, getting the kids involved, etc.), whereby they changed the form of the meetings and therefore also their culture.

It's obviously a question of taste, value orientation and culture internalized by the individual in choosing which variation of the parent-teacher meeting is most pleasant. At any rate, we see that the situation has the potential, if there is a willingness to change, to actively transform the structure and then culture. Yet the catalyst for changes was clearly a change in both class teachers which was of a cultural nature.

If we take the individual points from the wicked circle of causality that the teachers described, each part has this potential. If, for instance, they have the impression in schools that the kids rarely experience true democracy, the change in approach to how democratic the milieu at their school is can help. This can be linked to the issue of rules and coexistence among the kids themselves – a topic mentioned by teachers at both schools. We once again have before us an idea of the meanings linked to the given question – in this case to rules. From here there is a relatively short step to understanding that the kids need to learn how to create the rules themselves and to ensure that they observe them. For instance, a path to the supervisory work of a school parliament is offered as one of the possible structural solutions. The examples of schools who went through the process of a fundamental change of culture by setting up a school parliament can be greatly inspirational. Changes can also be made on other levels of the system.

There is, however, one catalyst necessary for a decision to make a change. In order to cross over from a wicked circle to an open system, the individual seeking the solution must avoid adapting to a closed system, and must be willing to fully accept freedom and assume responsibility for change. Yet it is the adaptability of teachers that has proven to be the most enduring quality during the transformation. Due to their experiences during the communist years, teachers are still used to adapting to the status quo. They are adept at being able to analyze the situation that they exist and work in. However, they often wait until the change comes from the outside world. Teachers feel that everything should change – the ministry, parents, kids, society... And even though I share a dissatisfaction with contemporary society, the way forward can't be made without exiting this wicked circle and taking things into one's own hands.

Examples from both schools show that the positive changes made at both schools had their inception within the system. They occurred thanks to individuals who had the courage to point out what was not working, took the initiative and responsibility and advanced the entire system. A path from the wicked circle leads to change when individuals refuse to adapt – a refusal to adapt to a bad system, to an aggressive hierarchy of values, to the unchecked demands of the work market; a refusal to support the dictate and instead to make the system better. Teachers have to find the courage for real freedom, so that they work as bold citizens in schools, as those with their own visions and assuming responsibility for the environment in which they work. They can turn from adapting enablers of a regime to revolutionaries of sorts. For the objective is clear, and teachers themselves have precisely named it: The goal is ultimately for "satisfied teachers, parents and children" to exist within the system. It may be true that children haven't changed since the days of Comenius, but the rest of the world has. And schools should react to this above all else.

Epilogue

After submitting the manuscript for final editing, several interesting things happened directly related to the subject of this book.

A week after submitting the manuscript I received an email from principal Hájek. He informed me in two sentences that he was being forced out of his job because two years before his retirement he hadn't taken part in the competition for his position that the town of Remízek had decided to announce in the spring of 2012. Nearly twenty years after Mr. Hájek had, under dramatic circumstances, replaced his colleague Mr. Brož as principal, he himself was being forced to 'leave' shortly before retirement. Once again a feeling of ingratitude and not being appreciated was evident. One acquaintance in the midst of choosing schools for his kids recently asked me what conclusions I had reached in my research. I began to cautiously talk of the symbols and rituals and that I felt that they had changed rather quickly and painlessly, although the same could not be said about the relations. My acquaintance got upset and began to shout: "What changes? The bells still ring, there are still lines for lunch and they still give the kids grades, report cards, nothing has changed!!!"

I explained that in the research I had focused more on political celebrations, special events during the year and that sort of thing. This somewhat placated him, but he insisted that nothing had changed on either a symbolic or ritualistic level.

Since I find myself in a similar situation of intensively choosing between primary schools for my kids, I keep holding an imaginary conversation with my acquaintance. Do I want bells to stop ringing in schools? Do I not want my kids to receive grades in the early years? Do my kids need a clearly structured system or more of a laxed approach that will awaken their imagination to a different kind of performance? Some parameters don't need a second thought, but in others I am searching with uncertainty just as my acquaintance, my respondents and the parents at the researched schools are. In this, we're all in the same boat.

Yet I feel that our/my inability to decide what we need does not come from these contemplations. Education in today's world faces a dramatic situation in which, although our entire society is knowledge-based, we don't actually know which skills our children will need in this rapidly changing world. My acquaintance noted that experts know that sixty percent of the professions in which our kids will work still don't exist. How then can we responsibly say what our kids will or won't need?

I feel that there is no answer to this question. And yet I believe that we aren't powerless. We can, along with our kids in our schools, search for new meanings and react to the challenges presented by today's world. But without good relations and trust this kind of process is not possible. It is for this, among other reasons, that I view the school milieu and its culture as a key parameter that should be the focal point of our work. Everything else will then come easier.

(Prague, 2010–2013)

Bibliography

Bahry, S. A. (2005). Travelling Policy and Local Spaces in the Republic of Tajikistan: a Comparison of the Attitudes of Tajikistan and the World Bank Towards Textbook Provision. *European Educational Research Journal,* 4, 60–78.

Banks, J. A. (ed.) (2004). *Diversity and Citizenship Education: Global Perspectives.* San Francisco: Jossey-Bass.

Beran, J. – Smékal, V. (1999). *Obecná škola v zrcadle pětiletého výzkumu.* Brno: Universitas Masarykiana Brunensis.

Berend, I. T. (2009). *From the Soviet Bloc to the European Union.* Cambridge: Cambridge University Press.

Burawoy, M. – Verdery, K. (eds.) (1999). *Uncertain Transition: Ethnographies of Change in the Postsocialist World.* Oxford: Rowman & Littlefield.

Cerych, L. (1997). Educational Reforms in Central and Eastern Europe: Processes and Outcomes. *European Journal of Education,* 32, 75–96.

Dahrendorf, R. (2005). *Reflections on the Revolution in Europe.* New Brunswick and London: Transaction Publishers.

Esteve, J. M. (2000). The Transformation of the Teachers' Role at the End of the Twentieth Century: New Challenges for the Future. *Educational Review,* 52, 197–207.

Fullan, M. (1996). Professional Culture and Educational Change. *School Psychology Review,* 25, 496–500.

Fullan, M. (2000). The Three Stories of Educational Reform. *Phi Delta Kappan International,* 81, 581–584.

Gardner, P. (2003). Oral History in Education: Teacher's Memory and Teacher's History. *History of Education,* 32, 175–188.

Giroux, H. A. – McLaren, P. (1989). *Critical Pedagogy, the State, and Cultural Struggle.* New York: State University of New York Press.

Goodson, I. F. (2005). *Learning, Curriculum and Life Politics.* London: Routledge.

Goodson, I. F. (2008). *Investigating the Teacher's Life and Work.* Rotterdam: Sense Publishers.

Goodson, I. F. – Hargreaves, A. (1996). *Teachers' Professional Lives*. London: Routledge.

Goodson, I. F. – Anstead C. J. (2012). *The Life of a School*. New York: Peter Lang.

Greger, D. (2011). Dvacet let českého školství optikou teorií změny vzdělávání v post-socialistických zemích. *Orbis scholae*, 1, 9–22.

Hargreaves, A. (1994). *Changing Teachers, Changing Times: Teachers' Work and Culture in the Postmodern Age*. London: Continuum International Publishing Group.

Higgins-D'Alessandro, A. – Sadh, D. (1998). The Dimensions and Measurement of School Culture: Understanding School Culture as the Basis for School Reform. *International Journal of Educational Research*, 27, 553–569.

Holmes, L. (1997). *Post-Communism: An Introduction*. Cambridge: Polity Press.

Jelínková, A. – Prusáková, V. (1988). *Občanská nauka pro 6. ročník základní školy*. Praha: SPN.

Jones, K. – Alexiadou, N. (2001) Travelling Policy: Local Spaces. Paper in the Global and the National: Reflections on the Experience of Three European States symposium, ECER, Lille, September.

Klaassen, C. (1992). The Latent Initiation: Sources of Unintentional Political Socialisation in the Schools. *Politics and the Individual*, 2, 41–65.

Kollmorgen, R. (2011). Transformationstheorien auf neuen Pfaden? Die Entwicklung der theoretisch-konzeptuellen Debatten über die postsozialistischen Umbrüche nach 1998/1999. *Berliner Journal für Soziologie*, 21, 295–319.

Konopásek, Z. (ed.) (2000). *Our Lives as Database: Doing a Sociology of Ourselves: Czech Social Transitions in Autobiographical Research Dialogues*. Prague: Nakladatelství Karolinum.

Kozakiewicz, M. (1994). The Difficult Road to Educational Pluralism in Central and Eastern Europe. *European Education*, 26, 25–35.

Kutsyuruba, B. (2011). Potential for Teacher Collaboration in Post-Soviet Ukraine. *International Journal of International Development*, 31, 547–557.

Kymlicka, W. (2001). *Politics in Vernacular: Nationalism, Multiculturalism and Citizenship*. Oxford: Oxford University Press.

Lansing, Ch. B. (2010). *From Nazism to Communism: German School Teachers under Two Dictatorships*. Cambridge, MA: Harvard University Press.

Miles, M. B. – Huberman M. A. (1994). *Qualitative Data Analysis: An Expanded Sourcebook*. London: Sage Publications.

Marková, I. (ed.) (2004). *Trust and Democratic Transition in Post-Communist Europe*. Oxford: Oxford University Press.

Moree, D. (2008). *How Teachers Cope with Social and Educational Transformation: Struggling with Multicultural Education in the Czech Classroom*. Benešov: Eman.

Oser, F. K. – Veugelers, W. (eds.) (2008). *Getting Involved: Global Citizenship Development and Sources of Moral Values*. Rotterdam: Sense Publishers.

Ozga, J. – Jones, R. (2006). Travelling and Embedded Policy: The Case of Knowledge Transfer. *Journal of Educational Policy*, 21, 1–17.

Peterson, K. D. – Deal, T. E. (2009). *The Shaping School Culture Fieldbook*. San Francisco: Jossey-Bass.

Pol, M. et al. (eds.) (2006). *Kultura školy: Příspěvek k výzkumu a rozvoji*. Brno: Masarykova Univerzita.

[anonymous]: Přijímací zkoušky na vysokou. *Listy*, 4, 1974, nos. 5–6, December, 5–6.

Seddon, T. (2005). Travelling Policy in Post-Socialist Education. *European Educational Research Journal*, 4, 1–4.

Szebenyi, P. (1992). Change in the System of Public Education in East Central Europe. *Comparative Education*, 28, 19–31.

Silova, I. (2005). Travelling Policies: Hijacked in Central Asia. *European Educational Research Journal*, 4, 50–59.

Sztompka, P. (1993). Civilizational Incompetence: The Trap of Post-Communist Societies. *Zeitschrift für Soziologie*, 22, 85–95.

Tomusk, V. (2001). Enlightenment and Minority Cultures: Central and East European Higher Education Reform Ten Years Later. *Higher Education Policy*, 14, 61–73.

Trahar, S. (ed.) (2009). *Narrative Research on Learning: Comparative and International Perspective*. Oxford: Symposium Books.

Tupý, K. – Vlčková, V. – Nečesaná, J. – Dušková, M. (1975). *Prvouka, didaktická a metodická kniha pro učitele*. Prague: SPN.

Ulč, O. (1978). Some Aspects of Czechoslovak Society Since 1968. *Social Forces*, 57, 419–435.

Urbášek, P. (2009). Vysokoškolští učitelé a vysokoškolské prostředí v letech tzv. normalizace. In: Vaněk (2009), 430–471.

Vaněk, M. (2009). *Obyčejní lidé...?! Pohled do života mlčící většiny: Životopisná vyprávění příslušníků dělnických profesí a inteligence*. Prague: Academia.

Vaněk, M. – Mücke, P. (2011). *Třetí strana trojúhelníku: Teorie a praxe orální historie*. Praha: Fakulta humanitních studií Univerzity Karlovy v Praze – Ústav pro soudobé dějiny AV ČR, v. v. i.

Veugelers, W. (2006). Democratie leren: Van der Hoeven en de Winter over onderwijs en burgerschapsvorming. *Pedagogische Studiën*, 83, 156–166.

Veugelers, W. – Derriks, M. – Ewoud de, K. (2006). Education and Major Cultural Incidents in Society: September 11 and Dutch Education. *Journal of Peace Education*, 3, 235–249.Veugelers, W. (2007). Creating Critical-Democratic Citizenship Education: Empowering Humanity and Democracy in Dutch Education. *Compare*, 37, 105–119.

Veugelers, W. (ed.) (2011). *Education and Humanism: Linking Autonomy and Humanity*. Rotterdam: Sense Publishers.

Walterová, E. – Greger, D. (2006). Transformace vzdělávacích systémů zemí vise-
-grádské skupiny: srovnávací analýza. *Orbis scholae*, 1, 13–29.
Westheimer, J. (2008). On the Relationship Between Political and Moral Engagement. In: Oser – Veugelers (2008).
Wong R. S. (1998). Multidimensional Influences of Family Environment in Education: The Case of Socialist Czechoslovakia. *Sociology of Education*, 71, 1–22.

Acts and documents

Czech Ministry of Education (2001). Bílá kniha (The White Book – The National
Developmental Plan for Education in the Czech Republic).
Czech Ministry of Education (1996). Vzdělávací program Základní škola (Prima-
ry School Educational Program). Multiple authors. Prague: Nakladatelství
Fortuna.
Czech Ministry of Education (1997). Vzdělávací program Národní škola (Na-
tional School Educational Program). Czech Association of Primary School
Teachers as part of the Czech Ministry of Education project. Prague: SPN.
Act 171/1990 Coll., which amends Act no. 29/1984 Coll., on primary and secon-
dary schools (the School Act).
Act 561/2004 Coll., on preschool, primary, secondary, tertiary and other educa-
tion. Prague: Institute for Information in Education – nakladatelství Tauris.

Summary

The process of transformation in Central and Eastern Europe is a multi-dimensional phenomenon. International literature suggests that a combination of changing structures and changing culture is indispensable for its success. However, what both literature and contemporary life in a transforming context show is that, while structures were changed relatively quickly, culture influenced by a totalitarian set of patterns continues to influence lives in these societies.

This basic idea was a starting point for the research presented in this book. Two schools and their teachers, pupils and parents in one mid-sized town in Central Bohemia were chosen for a three-year research project investigating the changes in school culture. The school environment was chosen for several reasons: Firstly, schools are microcosms of society – they consist of people living in one place, from different social and cultural backgrounds. Secondly, schools in particular were strongly linked to the previous regime – teachers were something like state agents who before 1989 had to transmit state ideology to their pupils. Logically, schools were also under great pressure to change after the collapse of communism in 1989. Thirdly, several generations of people converge in the school environment.

All these reasons led me to the decision to construct the research as follows: Teachers of two generations working in two schools in the town of Remízek were asked to participate in the research. Thirty-one teachers active in these two schools both before 1989 and at present were interviewed. These interviews were supplemented by focus groups with parents of children in the 6th grade in both schools and the School Culture Scale by Higgins-D'Alessandro – Sadh (1998) was used among pupils. Field research was complemented by document analysis and archive research.

Teachers in both schools view their professional lives as pre- and post-1989. When they describe the situation before 1989, they speak very much about the whole educational context. The reason was that teachers had to participate in a wide range of activities linked to ideological purposes, such as various political commissions, the Communist Party, etc. The fear of turning down an invitation to activities linked to the regime was too strong, consequently most teachers accepted the regime's requirements. Many teachers talked about dilemmas which accompanied their perception of the school environment before 1989. The more the decision was linked to the situation of specific pupils, the worse the dilemma was from the teachers' perspective – as, for instance, in the case of the personal assessment of pupils (known as the *kádrový posudek*).

The political changes of 1989 brought about a deterioration of relations in both schools. Although the course of this deterioration differed in each of the two schools, teachers talking about this period are unsure of how to evaluate it, even twenty years afterwards. The basic question of who is the hero and who is the traitor remains open.

Teachers perceive the situation after 1989 as ambivalent. The profound hope that the world really could change, which influenced life directly after 1989, has been replaced by disillusionment that the change has not happened that quickly and has not even brought about the expected improvements in the quality of life. Teachers reflect above all on the significant change in the value system, which they see as favoring individualism and market-driven values. An interesting aspect of this feeling is the chain of consequences we can distinguish in the teachers' argumentation. The changed value system in the society causes higher pressure on parents, who thus have less time for their children. Parents then have higher expectations of schools, but due to the lack of contact with parents, children are ruder in classes. This in turn has a negative impact on the teacher's role, which in turn makes teachers feel that their value system is totally different from the majority of society. This chain of consequences seems to be a vicious circle in the teachers' interviews.

However, teachers describing their experience with the transformation also seem to inhabit a vicious circle themselves. Teachers see themselves as victims of the communist regime, having been forced to accept circumstances dictated from outside. But their perception of this situation has not changed dramatically since 1989. It seems that teachers' conformism with regime requirements is the most stable feature of the transformation of school culture.

Teachers complain about their present situation regardless of the fact that the school system was radically decentralized after the school reform of 2004, which gives particular schools and teachers a unique opportunity to create a world where they would not be merely slaves of others' expectations. They might show what their real idea of a good school is.

But all of this requires teachers who are able to overcome the most difficult legacy of the communist regime – the susceptibility to conformism. Teachers might become real revolutionaries who could take responsibility for their world, represented by their school. If teachers were able to take their school's past seriously, learn more from their own experiences, see clearly the small successes they've achieved and learn from mistakes, they might also find new heroes, who would be able to give their school a new direction and who would be truly democratic, since they would be truly human.

Index

assessments 67–68, 70–72, 80, 166, 172

bullying 26, 130
bureaucrat 101

children 18, 19–23, 25, 31, 40–44,
    45–46, 49, 58–59, 65–66, 67–70,
    76–80, 88, 99, 101, 104, 110–112,
    118–122, 127–128, 135–137,
    142–144, 156, 161, 182–183,
    185–186, 191–192
civility 17, 25
culture 11, 12–15, 186, 188–190
– of the school 19, 24–27, 31, 36–37,
    115, 144, 174, 179
– toxic 27, 179
Czechoslovak Communist Party 19,
    20–21, 42, 48, 53–54, 56, 60, 62,
    64, 68, 69, 72, 88, 97, 173, 199
– membership in the Czechoslovak
    Communist Party 44, 47, 61,
    88–89, 99, 100, 102, 109, 167

degradation of education 117, 174,
    180, 185
dilemmas 21, 26, 28, 31–33, 74–79,
    82–83, 166, 169, 170–174,
    180–181, 199
discipline 185

disciplinary problems 182

educational system 18–25, 115, 117
expectations 15–16, 27, 32–33, 36,
    105, 111, 153–154, 159, 164,
    179–180, 182, 187, 199–200

general educational program (RVP)
    24, 116, 187

homework 133–134, 142, 155

meetings 19, 35, 53, 59–60, 70, 135,
    138, 140, 172, 189, 190
methods
– research 16, 25, 29, 30–31
– teaching 24, 77, 115, 119–120, 148,
    162, 169, 184, 188

parents 18, 20, 25, 31, 32, 34, 35–36,
    43, 47–48, 54, 55, 67–68, 70, 78,
    99, 109, 115, 125–127, 139–143,
    153–156, 160–161, 176–178,
    181–183, 189–190
Pioneers and Czechoslovak Socialist
    Union of Youth 68, 71, 75

reform 14, 24, 32, 33, 51, 115–119,
    122–124, 169, 174, 187

relations 15, 24, 26, 28, 31, 32, 35, 36,
    41, 70, 73, 78, 94, 97, 120, 123,
    132, 139, 147–148, 150–153, 162,
    167, 173, 175–177, 180–181, 185,
    189–190
– among kids 130–131, 142, 144
– among teachers 85–89, 92, 98, 108
– between teachers and kids 115, 127,
    134, 145
– between teachers and parents 115,
    135, 140, 143
restructuring 12, 18
rituals 14, 18, 25, 27, 51, 84, 147,
    174–175, 189
roles 18, 28, 64, 187
role of teachers 29, 159, 183
rules 55, 84, 110, 114, 134, 181, 187,
    190–191

school educational program (ŠVP)
    24, 116, 145, 184, 187
social differences 130, 151, 176

society 12, 13–19, 22, 25, 36, 56, 64,
    73, 76, 92, 100, 105, 109–115, 127,
    133, 140, 146, 153–154, 158, 162,
    164–166, 171, 173, 177, 179, 180,
    181–190
symbols 14, 18, 27, 28, 51, 85, 174–175,
    189, 192

training 39, 59, 60, 99, 114, 118,
    122–123, 126, 168, 172
transformation 10, 11–19, 21–22,
    23, 28, 31–32, 123, 134, 170, 174,
    179–180, 186, 189
travelling policy 23

values 14, 18, 21, 26–27, 78, 82, 102,
    104, 108, 110, 114, 136, 153, 158,
    162, 170, 177, 179, 181–184,
    187–190
value system 14, 109, 137, 177,
    180–181, 199

Dana Moree

Teachers on the Waves of Transformation
Czech School Culture
Before and After 1989

Published by Charles University
Karolinum Press
Ovocný trh 560/5, 116 36 Prague 1
Prague 2020
Designed by Jan Šerých
Typeset and printed by Karolinum Press
First English edition

ISBN 978-80-246-4377-9
ISBN 978-80-246-4417-2 (pdf)